CASSEROLES

Revised Edition

Christie Katona
Thomas Katona

BRISTOL PUBLISHING ENTERPRISES
San Leandro, California

A **nitty gritty**® Cookbook

Printed in the United States of America.

ISBN: 1-55867-265-6

Cover design: Frank J. Paredes
Cover photography: John A. Benson
Food stylist: Susan Devaty

CONTENTS

ALL ABOUT CASSEROLES

Casseroles evoke a homey, comforting and satisfying feeling. Everybody loves them for their savory smells, because they are perfect to make ahead of time, and because they are often a good way to use leftovers. Casseroles are a time-efficient, economical, nutritious and delicious way to feed a family. Besides being wonderful family fare, casseroles also make simple, casual entrées for guests.

Casserole is the name of the baking dish, and also the food it holds. Casseroles (the food) usually consist of cooked meats, poultry, fish, eggs and/or vegetables, some kind of liquid binder such as white sauce, tomato sauce or soup, and a topping of crumbs or other ingredients that offers texture and additional flavor. A casserole is baked in a glass, ceramic or metal baking container, often with a lid, that can also be used as the serving container. The most common casserole dish is deep and round—some authorities think this type cooks more evenly—but many are shallow, and some are square or rectangular. Some casseroles are cooked in Dutch ovens.

We have included Breakfast and Brunch Casseroles, International Favorites, and general categories like chicken, seafood, meats, side dishes and vegetables. For those in a real hurry, Soup-er Easy Casseroles and Can-Do Casseroles offer recipes made with off-the-shelf ingredients to get a great meal together in no time.
We hope you enjoy the recipes as much as our family has. Bon appétit!

CASSEROLE DISHES

Casserole dishes come in an amazing array of sizes, shapes, materials and decorative finishes. If you have limited space, you can get by with just a few basic dishes that work well for most casseroles.

Casseroles come in a wide assortment of materials: metal, enameled metal, glass, porcelain-coated iron, ceramic composites, and various combinations of these materials. If you are planning to purchase casserole dishes, we recommend that you purchase the best quality you can afford. Although more expensive initially, they will give you better results and will last a lifetime. You can even hand them down to your children when the time comes.

Enameled carbon-steel casseroles are ruggedly built and attractive, but are a little pricey. A clear glass lid allows the cook to check cooking progress without opening the lid. Cast-iron, enameled cast-iron and enameled carbon-steel pans are ideal for dishes which require sautéing on top of the range prior to baking in the oven. Stainless steel cookware is practically indestructible, doesn't react with food ingredients, and is easy to clean. Those made with an aluminum core between layers of stainless have solved the problem of hot spots which burn food. However, they also come at a higher price.

Perhaps the best compromise between price and quality are modern ceramic bake-and-serve dishes. Most are lightweight, dishwasher- and microwave-safe, and come in a wide variety of colors and patterns to dress up your table. One nice feature of this type of dish is the ability to easily reheat a casserole in the microwave.

Dutch ovens and Crock-Pots® or other slow cookers will work for some casseroles, but are generally more suited for dishes that are large and require long, slow simmering.

There are many casserole containers on the market from which to choose, from simple soufflé dishes to more exotic clay cookers or Moroccan tajine. You might find it fun to browse through a local kitchen shop and look at the varieties available.

Casseroles can be round, oval, square or rectangular and of any color and pattern. Many have matching lids and heat-proof handles. Square and rectangular dishes, assuming the depth to be between $1\frac{1}{2}$ and 2 inches, have the following approximate capacities:

7-x-10 inches	$1\frac{1}{2}$ quarts
7-x-11 inches	2 quarts
8-x-8 inches	$1\frac{1}{2}$ quarts
9-x-13 inches	$3-3\frac{1}{2}$ quarts
10-x-15 inches	5 quarts

To be certain of the capacity of your dish, use a graduated quart measuring cup and add water to the dish until you reach the desired depth. Round and oval casserole dishes are sold by their capacity (marked on the packaging). Use a dish that will hold your recipe with about ½ inch of clearance at the top for the best even heating.

GARNISHING

An attractive casserole dish and selective garnishes can greatly increase the overall appeal of your dinner. One easy way to garnish is to set aside one or several of the casserole ingredients, such as sliced mushrooms, olives or cheese. Sprinkle shredded cheese or cheese cut into interesting shapes on top of the dish. Plain, seasoned, or buttered breadcrumbs add a nice crunch and brown toasty texture to a dish. Cracker crumbs, crushed potato chips, crumbled crisp bacon, chow mein noodles or canned French-fried onion rings make tasty toppers. Refrigerated biscuit dough, dumplings and cornbread can provide appealing brown crusts.

To add color and flavor contrast, consider garnishing with the following items:

tomato wedges
lemon wedges
shredded lettuce
sliced green onions
pimientos

green olives stuffed with pimientos
a dollop of sour cream or plain yogurt
fresh parsley
sprigs of fresh herbs

Parsley makes an attractive, economical garnish for almost any dish. If you like to use parsley on a regular basis, wash a large bunch, wrap it in a paper towel and keep it in a closed glass jar in the refrigerator. The parsley will stay fresh for weeks and available for everyday cooking. A sprig of any fresh herb will dress up your creation. Many herbs grow easily in containers indoors near a sunny window.

STORAGE TIPS

You can make casseroles ahead of time or make more than one at a time and save the extras for future use. Casseroles can be frozen, but generally should be used within 2 months for best quality. To assure food safety, cool your casserole quickly, wrap tightly and freeze immediately. Wrap the casserole as tightly as possibly so that there is little air left in the bag or wrapping to draw moisture from the food. We generally use plastic wrap, and cover that with heavy-duty aluminum foil. Mark and date the packages so there won't be any surprises later. If you know you will be freezing a casserole, it is a good idea to undercook it slightly, so when it is reheated, it will not be overcooked. This is especially true for casseroles containing vegetables.

REDUCING FAT IN YOUR CASSEROLES

In the 50's, when casseroles were all the "rage," no one gave a second thought about adding sour cream, cheese, eggs and mushroom soup to their noodles and topping it all with buttered breadcrumbs. After all, that's what made them good.

Today, in a more diet-conscious society, we are often concerned about the amounts of fat, calories and cholesterol we consume. We have suggested "lighter" products in our recipes whenever possible. A myriad of new products are reduced fat, low fat, or nonfat in content. Products labeled reduced fat or low fat seem to be better tasting and work better in recipes than the nonfat items. Nonfat items and some low fat items often substitute moisture for the fattening ingredients, leaving too much liquid in the recipes. Carefully consider the labels and ingredients when substituting; however, for the most part, casseroles are pretty tolerant of a few changes here and there. Knudsen brand low-fat sour cream works well in casseroles and has a good flavor; Neufchatel cream cheese is a good substitute for cream cheese.

Using nonstick cooking spray instead of butter will eliminate some calories. Use nonstick pans with a minimum amount of butter or oil when sautéing onions and other vegetables. Add a little water, stock or wine to prevent scorching. Egg substitutes work well in many casseroles to reduce fat and cholesterol.

Campbell's has recently come out with two new types of the ever-popular cream soups: reduced fat and Healthy Choice cream of mushroom, cream of celery, and cream of chicken soups. These are just wonderful for casseroles!

Then again, some recipes are just not the same without the rich ingredients (you can occasionally splurge).

HEARTY MEAT CASSEROLES

BEEF AND BEAN BAKE

This can make a main dish to take to a potluck or a nice accompaniment for a barbecue.

1 lb. lean ground beef
1 onion, chopped
1 lb. bacon, cooked, drained and crumbled
1 can (31 oz.) pork and beans
1 can (27 oz.) red kidney beans, rinsed and drained
2 cans (15 oz. each) butter beans, rinsed and drained
2 tbs. molasses
1 tsp. dry mustard
1/2 cup ketchup
1/2 cup brown sugar, packed
1/2 cup water

Heat oven to 350°. Spray a 3-quart casserole with nonstick cooking spray. In a large skillet over medium-high heat, brown beef and onion until cooked through. Drain off any liquid. In large bowl, combine all ingredients. Pour into casserole and bake for 1 hour.

BEEF AND CORN CASSEROLE

Servings: 4-6

Children really like this quick-fix casserole.

1 lb. ground beef
1/2 cup chopped onion
1/2 cup chopped green bell pepper
1 can (16 oz.) whole tomatoes
1 can (8 oz.) tomato sauce
1 can (12 oz.) corn, drained
1 1/2 cup sliced pimiento-stuffed green olives
2 tsp. chili powder
1 cup coarsely crushed corn chips
1/2 cup shredded cheddar cheese, regular or low-fat

Heat oven to 325°. In a large skillet over medium-high heat, cook ground beef, onion and green pepper until beef is no longer pink and vegetables are softened. Drain off juices. Reserve 1/2 cup liquid from canned tomatoes and discard remainder. Coarsely chop whole tomatoes. Add to beef mixture with reserved tomato liquid, tomato sauce, corn, olives and chili powder. Spray a 1 1/2-quart casserole with nonstick cooking spray. Pour in meat mixture and top with crushed corn chips and cheese. Bake for 30 minutes.

SPINACH NOODLE CASSEROLE

Servings: 6-8

Sure to be a family favorite—just add a salad and hot bread and dinner is ready.

FILLING

1 pt. small curd cottage, regular or low-fat
1 pkg. (8 oz.) cream cheese or Neufchatel cheese
1/4 cup sour cream, regular or low-fat
1/3 cup chopped onion
1/3 cup chopped green bell pepper

To make filling, combine cream cheese, onion, green pepper, sour cream and cottage cheese with a food processor or by hand. Mixture should be well blended and there should be small chunks of onion and green pepper.

1 pkg. (8 oz.) spinach noodles
1 lb. lean ground beef, chicken or turkey
2 cans (8 oz. each) tomato sauce
1/2 cup grated Parmesan cheese

Heat oven to 350°. Spray a 2-quart casserole dish with nonstick cooking spray.
Cook noodles according to package instructions and drain well. Cook ground beef in a large skillet over medium-high heat until cooked through. Drain off any excess liquid. Add tomato sauce to meat and simmer. Place ½ of the noodles in the bottom. Spread with filling. Top with remaining noodles and pour meat mixture over the top. Sprinkle with Parmesan. Bake for 30 minutes or until bubbly.

BEEF AND BEER STEW

Just the thing for a winter's evening meal. Add a salad and some crusty bread and you're all set.

1/4 cup butter or margarine
2 1/2 cups sliced onions
4 lb. beef, cut into 1-inch cubes
2 tbs. flour
2 cups beer
1 tbs. vinegar

2 tsp. salt
1 tsp. pepper
1 tsp. sugar
2 bay leaves
1/2 tsp. crumbled dried thyme
3 tbs. minced fresh parsley

Heat oven to 350°. In a large Dutch oven over medium-high heat, melt butter and brown onions. Remove onions from pan and brown beef in drippings. Sprinkle with flour, add remaining ingredients, except parsley, and stir well. Cover with a tight-fitting lid and bake for 3 hours or until very tender. Remove bay leaves, sprinkle with parsley and serve.

BEEF AND MUSHROOMS WITH NOODLES

Servings: 6

This recipe can easily be doubled and is ideal for potluck suppers.

1 lb. lean ground beef
1 onion, chopped
2 cloves garlic, minced
½ lb. fresh mushrooms, sliced
1 tsp. salt
½ tsp. pepper
2 cans (8 oz. each) tomato sauce
1 can (15 oz.) creamed corn

1 cup tomato juice
1 pkg. (12 oz.) wide egg noodles,
   cooked and drained
8 oz. cheddar cheese, shredded,
   regular or low-fat
1 can (16 oz.) sliced ripe olives,
   drained, for garnish

Heat oven to 325°. Spray a 3-quart casserole with nonstick cooking spray. In a large skillet over medium-high heat, brown beef, onion, garlic and mushrooms until beef is cooked through. Drain off any excess liquid and season with salt and pepper. Add tomato sauce, corn and tomato juice. Combine with cooked noodles. Pour into casserole and sprinkle with cheese. Bake for 45 minutes. Top with sliced olives to garnish.

BEEF AND NOODLE CASSEROLE

Here's a family favorite, destined to become one of yours, too.

1 lb. lean ground beef or ground turkey
2 cloves garlic, minced
1 tsp. sugar
1 tsp. salt
1 can (15 oz.) tomato sauce
1 pkg. (3 oz.) cream cheese or Neufchatel cheese, room temperature
1/2 pt. sour cream, regular or low-fat
6 green onions, thinly sliced
12 oz. small egg noodles, cooked and drained
1 lb. shredded mozzarella cheese, regular or part skim

Heat oven to 350°. Spray a 9-x-13-inch casserole with nonstick cooking spray. In a large skillet over medium-high heat, brown meat. Drain off fat. Add garlic, sugar, salt and tomato sauce and turn heat to low. Simmer for 30 minutes. Combine cream cheese, sour cream and green onions in a small bowl. Layer 1/2 of the noodles in the casserole, cover with 1/2 of the cream cheese mixture and top with 1/2 of the mozzarella. Cover with meat sauce. Layer remaining noodles, cream cheese mixture and mozzarella. Bake for 30 minutes.

TEXAS HASH

We've been making this old favorite for years.

1 lb. lean ground beef
3 large onions, sliced
1 clove garlic, minced
1 green bell pepper, chopped
1 can (16 oz.) whole tomatoes with juice
1/2 cup uncooked rice
1 tsp. chili powder
2 tsp. salt
1/2 tsp. pepper

Heat oven to 350°. Spray a 2-quart casserole with nonstick cooking spray. In a large skillet over medium-high heat, brown beef, onions and garlic until meat is cooked and onions are soft. Add green pepper and cook until softened. In a large bowl, combine meat mixture with remaining ingredients. Cover casserole with a lid or foil and bake for 45 minutes. Remove lid and continue baking for 15 minutes longer.

VEAL AND PEPPERS WITH ORZO

The rice-shaped pasta, orzo, makes this a hearty dish.

2 medium red onions
1 large red bell pepper
1 large yellow bell pepper
1 large green bell pepper
3 tbs. olive oil
$1\frac{1}{2}$ lb. veal stew meat, cut into 1-inch cubes
$\frac{1}{3}$ cup dry vermouth
1 tbs. lemon juice
3 cups water
$1\frac{1}{2}$ tsp. salt
$\frac{1}{2}$ tsp. crumbled dried rosemary
$1\frac{1}{4}$ cups orzo
1 pkg. (9 oz.) frozen artichoke hearts, thawed
1 lemon, cut into wedges

Heat oven to 350°. Peel onions and cut into quarters. Cut peppers into 1-inch strips. In a large skillet over medium-high heat, heat oil and cook veal until well browned on all sides. Transfer to a shallow 3½-quart casserole. Add onion and peppers to skillet and cook until lightly browned. Place vegetables on top of veal. To pan drippings, add vermouth, lemon juice and water, scraping up any browned bits. Bring to a boil and pour over veal and vegetables. Sprinkle with salt and rosemary. Cover and bake for 1 hour. Remove lid and add orzo. Cover and continue baking for 30 minutes. Add artichoke hearts and continue baking until meat and orzo are tender, about 15 minutes. Garnish with lemon wedges.

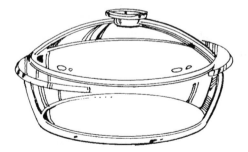

BRAISED VEAL WITH WINE SAUCE

This is one of those dishes that gets even better if you make it the day before and then reheat it just before serving. It also freezes well.

1/4 cup flour
1 tsp. salt
1/2 tsp. pepper
1 tsp. garlic powder
3 lb. veal stew meat, cut into 1-inch cubes
3 tbs. vegetable oil
3 large onions, chopped
2 carrots, grated
4 cloves garlic, minced
1/4 cup chopped green bell pepper
2 cans (16 oz. each) whole tomatoes with juice, chopped
1 can (8 oz.) tomato paste
1 cup dry white wine
1 tbs. sugar
1/2 tsp. crumbled dried basil
1/2 tsp. crumbled dried thyme
3 tsp. chicken stock base powder or chicken bouillon granules

Heat oven to 350°. Place flour, salt, pepper and garlic powder in a plastic bag. Shake veal cubes, a handful at a time, to coat. Heat oil in a heavy Dutch oven over medium-high heat, brown veal cubes in batches until golden. Drain off any excess juices. Place all ingredients in Dutch oven, cover tightly and bake for 2 hours or until veal is tender.

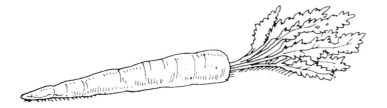

PECAN VEAL

Serve this rich and elegant entrée with rice pilaf to soak up the wonderful sauce.

1 1/2 lb. veal, cubed
1 tbs. vegetable oil
1 tbs. butter
1/2 cup water
1/4 cup chopped onion
1 tsp. chicken bouillon granules
1 clove garlic, minced
1/2 tsp. salt
1/2 tsp. dried thyme
1/4 tsp. dried oregano

Heat oven to 325°. In a heavy Dutch oven, brown veal cubes in oil and butter. Add remaining ingredients. Cover and bake for 1 hour or until veal is very tender. Drain off liquid into a measuring cup and add water to make 1 1/2 cups. Remove meat from Dutch oven and set aside. Place Dutch oven on burner over medium heat. Make sauce.

SAUCE

1 tbs. butter
1/4 cup chopped onion
1/2 cup chopped pecans
3 tbs. flour
1/2 cup sour cream, regular or low-fat

Melt butter and cook onion until tender. Add pecans and cook, stirring constantly, until golden. Blend flour into sour cream and stir in broth. Add to onion-nut mixture in pan; stir well.

Add veal and heat gently to thicken, but do NOT boil. Serve with rice or pasta.

VEAL WITH TOMATOES

Use Marsala wine to add depth of flavor to this light and flavorful dish. To peel a tomato easily, dip the tomato into boiling water for 30 to 45 seconds, remove and rinse with cold water. With a sharp paring knife, pierce the skin of the tomato and peel it. The skin will slip right off. Cut the tomato in half horizontally and squeeze the seeds out over the sink.

1 lb. veal cutlets
1/4 cup flour
1 tbs. olive oil
1 tbs. butter
1/2 cup Marsala wine or any white wine
1/2 lb. fresh mushrooms, sliced

1 cup chopped peeled, seeded, fresh
   tomatoes
1/4 cup grated Parmesan cheese
2 tbs. chopped fresh parsley
2 tbs. chopped fresh basil
1 tsp. garlic salt

Heat oven to 325°. Spray a 2-quart casserole with nonstick cooking spray. Pound veal with a meat mallet and dredge lightly in flour. Heat oil and butter in a large skillet over medium-high heat and cook veal until lightly browned on both sides. Place veal in casserole. Add wine to skillet and scrape up any crusty bits. Pour wine over veal and top with mushrooms, tomatoes, cheese and seasonings. Cover and bake for 45 minutes.

SAUSAGE STRATA

Use one of the new reduced-fat sausage mixtures to cut calories in this recipe.

15 slices day-old white bread, crusts removed
1 lb. pork sausage, cooked, drained and crumbled
1 small zucchini, diced
$\frac{1}{2}$ lb. fresh mushrooms, sliced
1 small onion, chopped
6 oz. cheddar cheese, shredded, regular or low-fat
1 qt. milk, whole or 2%
6 eggs, beaten, or egg substitute
1 tsp. salt
1 tsp. pepper

Spray a 9-x-13-inch casserole with nonstick cooking spray. Cut bread into $\frac{1}{2}$-inch cubes and spread evenly in casserole. Top with sausage, zucchini, mushrooms, onion and cheese. In a bowl, stir together milk, eggs, salt and pepper. Pour over casserole. Cover and refrigerate overnight.

Heat oven to 375°. Uncover casserole and bake for 1 hour.

SPINACH, HAM AND POTATO BAKE

To make spinach as dry as possible, thaw frozen spinach. Place it in a clean dish-towel and wring tightly over the sink to remove moisture. This casserole can be made a day ahead and is excellent for a potluck or brunch. It's a bright and color-ful way to serve leftover ham.

4 large potatoes, peeled and thinly sliced
½ lb. Swiss or low-fat Alpine Lace cheese, shredded
2 eggs, beaten
1 cup cream or evaporated skim milk
1 tsp. seasoning salt
½ tsp. pepper
1 pkg. frozen chopped spinach, thawed and
squeezed dry
1 medium onion, chopped
1 tbs. Dijon mustard
1 lb. baked ham, cut into strips
1 large red bell pepper, cut into strips

Heat oven to 325°. Spray a 3-quart casserole with nonstick cooking spray. Place ¹/₃ of the potatoes in the casserole and sprinkle with ¹/₃ of the cheese. Combine eggs, cream, seasoning salt and pepper. In a small bowl, combine spinach, onion and mustard. Spoon ¹/₃ of the egg and cream mixture over cheese and potato layer. Top with ham strips. Add second layer of potatoes and cheese and spoon another ¹/₃ of the egg and cream mixture over. Top with spinach and onion mixture. Add remaining ¹/₃ of the potatoes and cheese, drizzle with remaining egg and cream mixture and top with red pepper strips. Bake for 2 hours; do not cover. Top should be well browned. Cut into squares to serve.

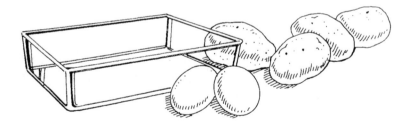

HAM AND CHICKEN CASSEROLE
WITH SWISS CHEESE

Servings: 6

This great luncheon dish freezes well. You can find ham that is almost fat-free.

1/2 cup chopped onion
1/2 lb. fresh mushrooms
2 tbs. butter or margarine
3 tbs. flour
1/2 tsp. salt
1/2 tsp. pepper
1 cup half-and-half
2 tbs. dry sherry

2 cups cubed cooked chicken or turkey
1 cup cubed cooked ham
1 can (8 oz.) sliced water chestnuts, drained
1 cup shredded Swiss or low-fat Alpine Lace cheese
1 1/2 cups soft breadcrumbs
3 tbs. butter or margarine, melted

Heat oven to 400°. Spray a 1 1/2-quart casserole with nonstick cooking spray. In a large skillet over medium heat, cook onion and mushrooms in butter until soft. Sprinkle with flour, salt and pepper. Add half-and-half and sherry. Cook until thickened. Add chicken, ham and water chestnuts. Pour mixture into casserole. Top with cheese. Combine crumbs and melted butter and sprinkle over top. Bake for 25 minutes or until bubbly and golden.

PORK AND RICE BAKE

Servings: 6

Start this casserole when the kids come home from school and by the time Dad walks in the door, dinner is ready. The aromas of this dish baking are delightful.

1 cup long-grain white rice, uncooked
1 can (1 lb. 2 oz.) whole tomatoes
1 can (6 oz.) tomato paste
1/2 cup diced green bell pepper
1/2 cup sliced celery
3/4 tsp. chili powder
1/2 tsp. dried oregano
1/2 tsp. garlic powder

1/2 tsp. salt
1/4 tsp. pepper
6 pork chops
1 tsp. salt
1 white onion, sliced horizontally into 6 slices
1 cup shredded cheddar cheese, regular or low-fat

Heat oven to 325°. Place uncooked rice in a shallow 3-quart casserole. Add tomatoes, tomato paste, green pepper and celery. Sprinkle with chili powder, oregano, garlic, 1/2 tsp. salt and pepper. Stir to mix together well. Trim any fat from pork chops and place in one layer on top of rice. Sprinkle with 1 tsp. salt. Top each chop with an onion slice. Cover tightly with a lid or foil. Bake for 1 hour and 15 minutes. Remove cover, sprinkle with cheese and return to oven to melt cheese, about 10 minutes longer.

PORK AND APPLES WITH MUSTARD CREAM SAUCE

Servings: 4-6

This dish is elegant enough for company. Serve with a salad, baby carrots and a rice pilaf. You need heavy cream so the sauce will thicken. You cannot accomplish this with half-and-half or milk. Don't worry—the cream won't burn.

2 lb. apples, peeled, cored and thinly
    sliced, prefer Golden Delicious,
    Granny Smith or Fuji
1 tbs. butter or margarine
6 pork chops, ¹/₂-inch thick

¹/₂ tsp. salt
¹/₄ tsp. pepper
¹/₄ cup dry white wine
1 cup whipping cream
¹/₃ cup Dijon mustard

Heat oven to 400°. Spray a 7-x-11-inch casserole with nonstick cooking spray. Layer apple slices in casserole and bake for 15 minutes. Heat butter in a large skillet over medium-high heat and brown chops on both sides. Sprinkle with salt and pepper. Arrange chops on top of apples. Add wine to pan drippings and stir up any browned bits. Cook until boiling. Add cream and mustard to skillet and cook until slightly thickened. Pour sauce over chops and apples, shaking casserole so sauce goes to bottom. Bake for 15 to 25 minutes or until chops are cooked through and tender.

WINTER CASSEROLE

This makes a simple, easy-to-fix dinner for a cozy evening at home. Just add a green salad and some hearty bread for a complete menu.

6 pork chops, about 1/2-inch thick
2 tbs. vegetable oil
2 red onions, cut into 1/2-inch-thick slices
4 Granny Smith apples, cored, unpeeled, and thickly sliced
1 tsp. chopped garlic
1 tsp. salt
1/2 tsp. pepper
1/2 cup apple juice or water, optional

Heat oven to 350°. In a large skillet over medium-high heat, brown chops in 1 tbs. of the oil. Cook until browned on both sides, about 2 minutes each side. Remove and set aside. In the same skillet, add remaining 2 tbs. oil and add onion slices and apples. Cook until brown on both sides. Place in an even layer in a shallow greased casserole. Sprinkle with garlic. Place browned chops on top and sprinkle with salt and pepper. Bake for 45 minutes, or until chops are tender. If you wish this dish to be more moist, sprinkle with apple juice or water and cook covered with a lid or foil.

CRANBERRY PORK CHOP BAKE

Servings: 4-8

This is a simple dish to assemble, but it tastes like you have really gone to a lot of trouble to fix it. A "zester" is a handy tool to remove the colored rind of the orange without any of the bitter white membrane underneath.

8 pork chops, ½-inch thick
1 can (15 oz.) whole berry cranberry sauce
grated zest and juice of 2 oranges

Heat oven to 425°. Spray a shallow 2-quart casserole with nonstick cooking spray. Place chops in bottom. In a small bowl, combine cranberry sauce, orange zest and juice. Pour over chops. Bake for 30 to 40 minutes or until chops are glazed and meat is cooked through.

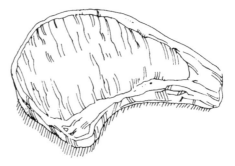

EASY PORK CHOP BAKE

Add some potatoes to bake in the oven at the same time and dinner is all set.

6 pork chops, 1-inch thick
salt and pepper to taste
6 thin slices onion
6 thin slices lemon
$1/3$ cup brown sugar
$1/3$ cup ketchup

Heat oven to 350°. Spray a shallow 3-quart casserole with nonstick cooking spray. Arrange pork chops in casserole. Sprinkle with salt and pepper. Top each chop with a slice of onion, a slice of lemon, a sprinkle of brown sugar and a tablespoon of ketchup. Cover pan with foil or lid, bake for 1 hour, uncover and continue baking for 30 minutes.

PORK CHOPS WITH ORANGE RAISIN SAUCE

Servings: 6

If you wish, stuff the pork chops with a bread stuffing before adding the sauce.

6 thick-cut pork chops
1 tbs. vegetable oil

ORANGE RAISIN SAUCE

1 cup raisins
1 cup water
1/3 cup brown sugar, packed
1 1/2 tbs. cornstarch
1/4 tsp. cinnamon
1/4 tsp. dry mustard

1/4 tsp. ground cloves
1/4 tsp. salt
1 cup orange juice
2 tbs. butter
1 tbs. cider vinegar

Heat oven to 350°. Spray a shallow 2-quart casserole with nonstick cooking spray. In a large skillet over medium-high heat, brown pork chops in oil. Place pork chops in casserole. In a saucepan, boil raisins in water for 5 minutes. Drain raisins. Combine brown sugar, cornstarch and seasonings in a small bowl. Add orange juice and dry ingredients to raisins. Reduce heat and cook for 10 minutes. Stir in butter and vinegar. Pour over pork chops and bake for 40 minutes.

PORK AND CABBAGE CASSEROLE

Servings: 6

The aroma of this dish cooking is heavenly. Even kids who aren't fond of cabbage like this casserole.

6 pork chops, about 1/2-inch thick
2 tbs. vegetable oil
4 large potatoes, peeled and sliced
1 large onion, chopped
1 tsp. salt
1/2 tsp. pepper
4 cups coarsely chopped green cabbage
1 can (10 1/2 oz.) cream of mushroom soup, regular or low-fat

Heat oven to 350°. In a heavy Dutch oven, heat oil over medium-high heat. Brown chops on both sides, about 3 minutes each side. Remove and set aside. Layer potatoes in pan and top with onion. Sprinkle with salt and pepper. Top with chops and cabbage. Pour soup over top. Bake for 1 1/2 hours.

CHICKEN AND SEAFOOD CASSEROLES

QUICK CHICKEN PARMESAN

There are many really good prepared spaghetti sauces available at the grocery store. Choose your favorite one to make this delicious Italian recipe. Serve with a side dish of simple boiled pasta, Caesar salad and garlic bread.

1 egg
1 tsp. water
1/4 tsp. salt
1 cup breadcrumbs
1/2 cup grated Parmesan cheese
6 boneless, skinless chicken breast
halves

3 tbs. olive oil
1 jar (16 oz.) prepared spaghetti sauce
6 oz. shredded mozzarella cheese,
regular or part skim
1/4 cup grated Parmesan cheese

Heat oven to 350°. Spray a shallow 1 1/2-quart casserole with nonstick cooking spray. Combine egg, water and salt in a shallow dish. Combine crumbs and 1/2 of the Parmesan in a second shallow dish. Dip chicken in egg mixture and roll in crumbs. Heat oil in a large skillet over medium-high heat and brown chicken breasts on both sides. Arrange chicken pieces in casserole and cover with spaghetti sauce. Bake for 45 minutes. Top with cheeses and continue to bake for 10 minutes longer.

LEMON CHICKEN

This dish is easily doubled and is good hot or cold.

3 lb. chicken pieces of your choice
1 cup lemon juice
1 cup flour
1 tsp. salt
1/2 tsp. pepper
1 tsp. paprika

1/3 cup vegetable oil
1 tbs. grated lemon zest
2 tbs. brown sugar
1/4 cup chicken broth
1 tsp. lemon extract
1 lemon, thinly sliced

Marinate chicken pieces in lemon juice overnight.

Heat oven to 350°. Spray a 9-x-13-inch casserole with nonstick cooking spray. Drain chicken and pat dry with paper towels. Combine flour, salt, pepper and paprika in a plastic bag and shake chicken pieces to coat. Heat oil in a large skillet and fry chicken over medium heat until brown and crisp, about 5 minutes on each side. Place chicken in a single layer in casserole. Sprinkle with lemon zest and brown sugar. Combine chicken broth and lemon extract and pour over chicken. Place lemon slices on top of chicken. Bake for 30 to 40 minutes, or until chicken is tender.

ZESTY CHICKEN BAKE

Use a mixture of breasts and thigh portions or chicken quarters to make this dish.

8 chicken pieces
1 pkg. (1.5 oz.) dry onion soup mix
1 bottle (8 oz.) red Russian dressing
1 cup apricot jam

Heat oven to 375°. Spray a 3-quart casserole with nonstick cooking spray. In a bowl, stir together onion soup mix, dressing and jam until combined. Arrange chicken pieces in casserole. Pour sauce over. Bake for 1 hour; baste occasionally with sauce.

CHICKEN AND BROCCOLI SUPREME

Servings: 6-8

We have had this excellent recipe in our repertoire for over 30 years. It makes an elegant entrée for a dinner party. Choose light accompaniments to this rich dish.

4 whole chicken breasts
water to cover
1 tbs. soy sauce
1 tbs. Worcestershire sauce
1 tsp. garlic powder
2 pkg. (10 oz. each) frozen broccoli spears
1 pkg. (1.5 oz.) dry onion soup mix
1 pt. sour cream, regular or low-fat
1 cup whipping cream, whipped
1/4 cup shredded Parmesan cheese

Place chicken in a large pan, cover with water and add soy sauce, Worcestershire and garlic powder. Bring to a boil, reduce heat and simmer until chicken is cooked, about 25 minutes. Drain and let cool. Remove skin and bones and cut meat into large pieces.

Heat oven to 350°. Spray a 3-quart casserole with nonstick cooking spray. Cook broccoli briefly until just tender, rinse with cold water to stop cooking and drain well. Arrange cooked broccoli in a single layer in casserole. Top with chicken. Combine sour cream and soup mix. Fold in whipped cream. Pour sauce over chicken and broccoli and top with Parmesan. Bake for 20 minutes.

CHICKEN ROMANO

Serve this colorful and flavorful dish with pasta or rice.

3 whole chicken breasts
1 tsp. salt
$\frac{1}{2}$ tsp. pepper
1 tbs. olive oil
2 red bell peppers, cut into strips
1 green bell pepper, cut into strips
4 cloves garlic, minced
$\frac{1}{4}$ cup grated Parmesan cheese

Heat oven to 325°. Spray a 1$\frac{1}{2}$-quart casserole with nonstick cooking spray. Place chicken breasts on a rimmed baking sheet and bake for 45 minutes. Cool. Remove skin and bones from chicken breasts, leaving pieces in large chunks. Place chicken in casserole and season with salt and pepper. Heat oil in a large skillet over medium-high heat and cook peppers and garlic for 5 minutes or until softened. Pour over prepared chicken and sprinkle with Parmesan. Bake for 15 to 20 minutes, or until piping hot.

PLUM SAUCE CHICKEN

This flavorful glaze uses plum sauce and lemonade concentrate to create a delicious sweet-and-sour sauce. Plum sauce is available in the Oriental food section of your grocery store.

4 whole chicken breasts, skinned,
  boned and halved
2 tbs. vegetable oil
1/4 cup finely chopped onion
1 clove garlic, minced
2 tsp. grated fresh ginger

1/3 cup plum sauce
1/4 cup frozen lemonade concentrate
1/4 cup chili sauce
2 tbs. soy sauce
1 tbs. lemon juice
1 tsp. dry mustard

In a large skillet over medium-high heat, brown chicken in oil. Remove chicken and place in a shallow baking dish. Preheat oven to 350°. Pour off all but 1 tbs. fat from skillet. Add onion, garlic and ginger and cook until onion is softened. Add remaining ingredients to the pan and stir to blend well. Reduce heat and simmer for 5 minutes. Pour over chicken and bake for 30 to 40 minutes, basting occasionally with sauce.

COUNTRY CHICKEN AND VEGETABLES

Servings: 6-8

Just add crusty bread and a green salad for a light yet hearty dinner.

2 whole chicken breasts, split
4 chicken thighs
2 cloves garlic, minced
1 onion, chopped
2 tbs. butter
1/2 cup diced green bell pepper

2 carrots, thinly sliced
3 tomatoes, seeded and chopped
1 tsp. salt
1/2 tsp. pepper
1 tsp. paprika
1 can (10 1/2 oz.) fat-free chicken broth

Heat oven to 325°. Place chicken pieces in a single layer on a rimmed baking sheet that has been sprayed with nonstick cooking spray. Bake chicken for 45 minutes, basting occasionally with pan juices. In a large skillet, cook garlic and onion in butter until softened. Add green pepper, carrots, tomatoes, seasonings and chicken broth. Simmer for 20 minutes. Remove chicken from baking sheet and place in a shallow 3-quart casserole. Pour vegetables and broth over chicken. Bake until chicken is cooked through and very tender, about 30 to 40 minutes.

OLD-FASHIONED SCALLOPED OYSTERS

This has become a holiday favorite for us.

1 qt. oysters
1 tbs. minced fresh parsley
1 tbs. minced celery
1 tbs. minced onion
$\frac{1}{2}$ tsp. salt
$\frac{1}{4}$ tsp. pepper
$1\frac{1}{2}$ cups crushed soda crackers
2 eggs, beaten
3 cups milk
2 tbs. butter or margarine

Heat oven to 325°. Spray a shallow $1\frac{1}{2}$-quart casserole with nonstick cooking spray. Arrange oysters in casserole and sprinkle with parsley, celery, onion, salt and pepper. Top with cracker crumbs. Beat eggs and milk together and pour over top. Dot with butter. Bake for 30 minutes.

SHRIMP AND CHEESE STRATA

Servings: 6

Stratas are similar to soufflés, but much less temperamental. In this version, sour cream adds a special tang.

6 slices firm white bread, crusts removed
1/4 cup butter or margarine, melted
1 cup shredded Swiss or low-fat Alpine lace cheese
2 green onions, thinly sliced
2 tbs. chopped fresh parsley

1/2 lb. bay shrimp
3 eggs, beaten, or egg substitute
1/2 cup sour cream, regular or low-fat
1 1/2 cups milk, whole or 2%
1/2 tsp. seasoning salt
1 tsp. Dijon mustard

Cut each slice of bread in half on the diagonal to form a triangle. Drizzle each slice with melted butter. Arrange 1/2 of the slices in an unbuttered 8-inch baking dish. Sprinkle with 1/2 of the cheese, onions, parsley and shrimp. Add remaining bread and repeat. Beat eggs with sour cream, milk and seasonings. Pour over casserole. Cover and refrigerate overnight.

Heat oven to 350°. Bake casserole for 30 to 40 minutes or until puffed and golden. Cut into squares to serve.

SHRIMP ROCKEFELLER

Servings: 4

A very elegant recipe! It's supposedly named Rockefeller because it's so rich. To really steal the show, add some crumbled crisp bacon with the breadcrumbs.

1 pkg. (10 oz.) frozen chopped
    spinach, cooked and well-drained
1 cup sour cream, regular or low-fat
1 tsp. horseradish
1/2 cup ketchup
1/2 tsp. onion powder
1 tsp. parsley flakes

1 tsp. lemon juice
1 tsp. salt
1/2 tsp. pepper
1 1/2 lb. cooked fresh shrimp
1 cup breadcrumbs
2 tbs. butter or margarine, melted

Heat oven to 450°. Spray a 1 1/2-quart casserole with nonstick cooking spray. Combine well-drained spinach with sour cream and seasonings. Mix well. Gently fold in shrimp. Pour into prepared casserole. Top with crumbs and drizzle with butter. Bake for 15 to 20 minutes or until bubbly and top is browned.

HOT SEAFOOD SALAD

This recipe has been a family favorite for years. Miracle Whip has ¹/₃ the calories of mayonnaise and makes a nice tangy sauce for this dish. Use less if you prefer.

2³/₄ cups uncooked sea shell macaroni
1 cup fresh bay shrimp
1 cup fresh crabmeat
1 can (6 oz.) tuna packed in water, well drained
1 green bell pepper, chopped

2 hard-cooked eggs, chopped
1 pt. Miracle Whip brand salad dressing, or less
¹/₂ cup fine breadcrumbs
2 tbs. butter or margarine, melted
¹/₂ tsp. paprika

Spray a shallow casserole with nonstick cooking spray. Cook pasta in boiling salted water until tender. Drain and refresh with cold water. Combine cooked pasta and seafood, green pepper, eggs and Miracle Whip. Place in casserole, cover and refrigerate overnight.

The next day, heat oven to 475°. Sprinkle top with breadcrumbs, drizzle with butter and sprinkle with paprika. Bake for 15 minutes.

CRAB BAKE

Almost like a crustless quiche, this casserole makes a nice brunch or luncheon entrée. Serve with a green salad, crusty bread and white wine for easy elegance.

2 tbs. butter or margarine
1/2 lb. fresh mushrooms, sliced
4 eggs or egg substitute
1 cup sour cream, regular or low-fat
1 cup small curd cottage cheese, regular or low-fat
1/2 cup freshly grated Parmesan cheese

1/4 cup flour
1 tsp. onion powder
1/2 tsp. salt
4 drops Tabasco Sauce
2 cups shredded Monterey Jack cheese, regular or low-fat
1 lb. fresh crabmeat

Heat oven to 350°. Spray a 1 1/2-quart casserole with nonstick cooking spray. Melt butter in a large skillet over medium-high heat and cook mushrooms until tender. In a large bowl, whisk together remaining ingredients, except cheese and crabmeat, until blended. Add mushrooms, cheese and crabmeat. Pour mixture into casserole and bake for 45 minutes. Let stand for 5 minutes before serving.

DEVILED CRAB

Servings: 4

Rich, delicious — and expensive! a quick treat to make on payday. Serve with green salad and a dry white wine.

4 slices fresh bread
¾ cup half-and-half
8 oz. fresh crabmeat
2 tbs. finely diced celery
2 tbs. finely diced green bell pepper
1 tbs. finely diced onion

1 tbs. finely chopped pimiento
1 tsp. dry mustard
½ tsp. salt
½ tsp. Worcestershire sauce
½ cup fresh breadcrumbs
2 tbs. butter or margarine, melted

Heat oven to 350°. Spray a 1-quart casserole with non-stick cooking spray. Soak bread in half-and-half until soft. In a bowl, combine bread, crabmeat, chopped vegetables and seasonings. Pour into prepared casserole. Top with fresh crumbs and drizzle with butter. Bake for 20 minutes or until bubbly and crumbs are golden.

BAKED CRAB AND EGG SALAD

Servings: 6

A spinach salad with poppy seed dressing accented with avocado and grapefruit slices would complement this entrée perfectly. Always pick over crabmeat to remove any bits of cartilage or shell. Evaporated skim milk has a nice smoothness and makes a lower calorie substitute for half-and-half.

1 1/2 cups mayonnaise
1 can (8 oz.) sliced water chestnuts, drained
1 tbs. thinly sliced green onion
1/4 tsp. seasoning salt
1/4 tsp. pepper
1 cup half-and-half or evaporated skim milk
1 tbs. finely minced fresh parsley
7 hard-cooked eggs, mashed
2 cups fresh crabmeat

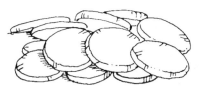

Heat oven to 350°. Spray a shallow 1 1/2-quart casserole with nonstick cooking spray. Combine all ingredients in a bowl. Transfer to casserole and bake for 30 minutes. Let stand for 10 minutes before serving.

CRAB AND SHRIMP CASSEROLE

Servings: 8

This is one of our all-time favorites, perfect for impressing guests.

1 cup uncooked white rice
3 tbs. butter or margarine
3 tbs. flour
1 1/2 cups milk, whole or 2%
1 tsp. Worcestershire sauce
3 drops Tabasco Sauce
1/2 tsp. salt
1/4 tsp. pepper
1 green bell pepper, chopped

1 onion, chopped
2 tbs. butter or margarine
1 can (8 oz.) sliced water chestnuts, drained
1 cup mayonnaise
1 lb. bay shrimp
1 lb. crabmeat
2 cups shredded cheddar cheese, regular or low-fat

Heat oven to 350°. Spray a 2-quart shallow casserole with nonstick cooking spray. Cook rice according to package directions and place in prepared casserole. Melt butter in saucepan over medium-high heat and whisk in flour. Add milk and cook until thickened and bubbly. Add seasonings. Add to rice. Melt remaining butter in a skillet over medium-high heat and cook green pepper and onion until soft. Stir into rice and sauce with water chestnuts, mayonnaise, shrimp and crabmeat. Top with cheese. Bake for 30 minutes.

SEAFOOD CASSEROLE

Here's a delicious way to stretch a small amount of expensive seafood. Use any small shaped pasta you like—there are so many interesting ones available.

1 1/2 cups uncooked shell macaroni
1 pkg. (8 oz.) cream cheese or
  Neufchatel cheese, softened
1/2 cup sour cream, regular or low-fat
1/2 cup cottage cheese, regular or low-
  fat
1/4 cup thinly sliced green onions
1 clove garlic, minced

1/4 tsp. salt
1/2 lb. bay shrimp
1/2 lb. fresh crabmeat
1 cup sliced fresh mushrooms
1 large tomato, sliced
2 cups shredded cheddar cheese,
  regular or low-fat

Heat oven to 350°. Spray a 1 1/2-quart shallow casserole with nonstick cooking spray. Cook macaroni according to package directions. Drain and layer 1/2 of the macaroni in casserole. Mix cream cheese, sour cream, cottage cheese, onions, garlic and salt. Spread 1/2 of the cheese mixture on top of macaroni and top with shrimp, crabmeat and mushrooms. Add remaining macaroni, remaining cheese mixture and sliced tomato. Top with shredded cheddar cheese. Bake for 30 minutes or until bubbly.

ITALIAN BAKED FISH

Here's a very colorful and easy way to serve fish. Sole, flounder, orange roughy or cod work well for this dish.

4 fresh tomatoes, sliced
1 cup seasoned Italian breadcrumbs
1 lb. fish fillets
1 tsp. salt
1/2 tsp. pepper
1/2 cup white wine

1/4 cup butter or margarine
1 tsp. lemon juice
1/2 cup grated Parmesan cheese
1 tbs. minced fresh parsley
paprika
lemon wedges for serving

Heat oven to 400°. Spray a 9-x-13-inch casserole with nonstick cooking spray. Line bottom of dish with tomato slices. Sprinkle with 1/2 of the breadcrumbs. Arrange fish in a single layer over mixture and sprinkle with salt and pepper. Combine wine, butter and lemon juice in a saucepan, bring to a boil and cook for 3 minutes. Pour over fish. Sprinkle with remaining breadcrumbs, Parmesan and parsley. Dust with paprika. Bake for 10 to 20 minutes, or until fish flakes with a fork. Serve with lemon wedges.

SOUR CREAM BAKED FISH

Almost any type of white fish can be prepared this way—halibut, shark, sword-fish or red snapper. Serve with a green vegetable and red-skinned potatoes.

2 lb. fish fillets
1 cup dry white wine
1 tsp. salt
1 cup mayonnaise
1/2 cup sour cream or plain yogurt
1 tsp. Dijon mustard

3 green onions, thinly sliced
1 cup fresh breadcrumbs
1/2 cup grated Parmesan cheese
paprika
lemon wedges for serving

Spray a shallow 1 1/2-quart casserole with nonstick cooking spray. Place fish in casserole and pour white wine over fish. Sprinkle with salt. Cover and refrigerate for several hours. Mix mayonnaise, sour cream, mustard and green onions. Pour wine off fish and discard.

Heat oven to 450°. Spread mayonnaise mixture over fish and sprinkle with breadcrumbs, Parmesan and paprika. Bake for 20 minutes, or until fish flakes and is opaque in the center. Serve with lemon wedges.

CHILEAN SEA BASS VEGETABLE BAKE

Servings: 4

The beautiful colors and lovely aroma make this casserole a winner. It can be assembled early in the day and refrigerated until ready to bake. Use low-fat margarine to cut calories even more.

1/4 cup butter or margarine
4 tsp. finely chopped fresh basil
2 cloves garlic, minced
2 tbs. lemon juice
4 red-skinned new potatoes

8 baby carrots
8 slender asparagus spears
1 1/2 lb. fresh boneless Chilean sea bass fillets

Heat oven to 425°. Spray a shallow 3-quart casserole or a 9-x-13-inch casserole dish with nonstick cooking spray. Combine butter, basil, garlic and lemon juice in a small bowl until well mixed. Parboil potatoes and baby carrots for 5 minutes, drain and pat dry. Divide fish fillets into 4 portions. Place fillets in casserole and arrange vegetables over fish in an attractive pattern. Top each fish portion with 1/4 of the garlic butter mixture. Cover dish tightly with foil or a lid. (Can be refrigerated at this point.) Bake for 25 to 35 minutes or until fish flakes easily with a fork. Serve immediately.

INTERNATIONAL FAVORITES

EASY MOUSSAKA

To remove the bitterness from eggplant, peel and slice. Place in a single layer on paper towels and sprinkle both sides with salt. Let stand for 30 minutes. Blot dry with paper towels and proceed with your recipe. This dish freezes well.

3 medium eggplants, peeled and cut
   into ½-inch slices
3 tbs. butter or margarine
3 tbs. vegetable oil
2 lb. lean ground lamb or beef
3 large onions, chopped
3 tbs. tomato paste
½ cup dry red wine
½ cup chopped fresh parsley
½ tsp. cinnamon

2 tsp. salt
1 tsp. pepper
½ cup butter or margarine
⅓ cup flour
1 qt. milk
4 eggs, beaten
1 pt. ricotta cheese, regular or low-fat
nutmeg
1 cup fine breadcrumbs
1 cup freshly grated Parmesan cheese

Sprinkle both sides of eggplant slices with salt and place in a single layer on paper towels. Let stand for 30 minutes. Blot dry with paper towels.

Melt butter and oil in a heavy skillet over medium-high heat. Brown eggplant slices in batches, setting them aside as they are browned. In pan drippings, cook lamb and onions until meat is crumbly and onions are soft. Drain off any excess liquid. Add tomato paste, wine, parsley and seasonings to the pan. Cook until mixture thickens. Remove from heat and set aside.

Make a white sauce by melting $\frac{1}{2}$ cup butter in a medium saucepan over medium high heat. Whisk in flour and stir for several minutes until smooth. Heat milk separately in a pan or in the microwave. Whisk milk into flour mixture and stir until bubbly, thickened and smooth. Remove from heat and let cool. Stir in eggs and ricotta; add nutmeg to taste.

Heat oven to 375°. Spray an 11-x-16-inch casserole, about 3 inches deep, with nonstick cooking spray. Layer eggplant and meat in casserole, sprinkling each layer with breadcrumbs and Parmesan; repeat. Pour ricotta cheese sauce over the top. Bake casserole, uncovered, for 1 hour. Let stand for 10 minutes before cutting into squares.

ZUCCHINI AND TURKEY MOUSSAKA

Servings: 8-10

This is a lighter version of the traditional Greek dish, which uses lamb and egg-plant. This variation is perfect when your garden gets overly zealous with the zucchini crop. It can be made ahead and refrigerated or frozen.

2 lb. zucchini, unpeeled, cut into 1-inch slices
3 large onions, chopped
1 tbs. olive oil
2 lb. ground turkey
2 cloves garlic, minced
1 can (16 oz.) stewed tomatoes, chopped
1 can (8 oz.) tomato sauce
1 tsp. salt
1/2 tsp. pepper
1 tsp. dried basil
1 tsp. dried oregano
1 lb. low-fat ricotta cheese
1 pkg. (8 oz.) Neufchatel cheese
1 cup breadcrumbs
1/2 cup grated Parmesan cheese

Heat oven to 400°. Place zucchini slices on a rimmed jelly-roll pan which has been sprayed with nonstick cooking spray. Cover with foil and bake until zucchini is soft, about 10 minutes. Remove from oven and set aside.

Set oven heat to 350°. Spray a 3-quart shallow casserole with nonstick cooking spray. In a large skillet, sauté onions in oil until they begin to soften; add turkey and garlic. Cook until turkey is no longer pink and onion is softened. Pour off any excess liquid. Add tomatoes, tomato sauce and seasonings to turkey and simmer for 5 minutes. In a bowl, combine ricotta and cream cheese until blended. Spread $1/3$ of the meat sauce on the bottom of casserole, top with $1/2$ of the zucchini slices, and add another $1/3$ of the meat sauce and $1/2$ of the ricotta mixture. Repeat with remaining sauce, zucchini and ricotta mixture. Sprinkle top with crumbs and Parmesan. Bake for 35 minutes or until piping hot.

STUFFED PEPPERS GREEK-STYLE

Here is a variation of the traditional stuffed pepper recipe. Fresh herbs add zing.

8 large green bell peppers
2 tbs. olive oil
1 small onion, chopped
1 clove garlic, minced
2 tomatoes, chopped
2 lb. lean ground lamb
1 can (6 oz.) tomato paste
2 tbs. chopped fresh parsley
2 tbs. chopped fresh mint

$1/4$ cup raisins
$1 1/2$ cups cooked rice
2 tsp. salt
$1/4$ tsp. pepper
$1/4$ cup olive oil
juice of 1 small lemon
1 cup tomato juice
1 tbs. flour

Heat oven to 350°. With nonstick cooking spray, spray a casserole large enough to hold peppers. Slice tops from peppers and remove seeds. In a large skillet, heat oil and cook onion, garlic and tomatoes for 10 minutes. Remove from heat and add lamb, tomato paste, parsley, mint, raisins, rice, salt and pepper. Blend well and stuff into peppers. Place peppers in casserole. Blend remaining ingredients together and spoon over peppers. Bake for 45 minutes or until meat is cooked; baste occasionally with pan juices.

MIDDLE EASTERN OVEN LAMB CURRY

Servings: 6

Traditionally curry is served over a bed of steamed rice. Condiments to accompany the curry are placed in small dishes around the platter. Some ideas to try include chutney, pickles, sliced green onions, peanuts, cashews, coconut, chopped hard-cooked egg, chopped tomato, raisins, pineapple chunks and crumbled bacon. Guests help themselves to toppings of their choice to create personal curries.

2 lb. lamb, cut into 3/4-inch cubes
1 cup water
1/2 cup ketchup
1 tsp. grated fresh orange zest
1 orange, peeled and sectioned, seeds removed
1 onion, chopped

2 cloves garlic, minced
1 cup raisins
1/2 cup chopped apple
1 tbs. curry powder
1 tsp. salt
1/2 tsp. ground ginger

Heat oven to 325°. In a 2-quart casserole with a tight-fitting lid, mix together all ingredients. Bake covered for 2 to 3 hours, or until meat is very tender.

GREEK LAMB PASTITSIO

Three different parts make up this delicious casserole. Although the recipe might seem complex, do try it. All of the parts can be made in advance, assembled and then refrigerated.

2 tbs. olive oil
1 onion, chopped
3 cloves garlic, minced
1 lb. lean ground lamb
1 1/2 cups tomato sauce
1/4 cup minced fresh parsley
1/2 tsp. crumbled dried rosemary
1/4 tsp. cinnamon
1 tsp. salt
1/2 tsp. pepper
1/4 cup butter or margarine

2 tbs. flour
1 1/2 cups milk
2 eggs, beaten
1/4 cup freshly grated Parmesan cheese
1 pinch nutmeg
8 oz. dried ziti pasta, cooked and drained
1 cup grated Monterey Jack cheese, regular or part skim
additional nutmeg

Heat oven to 375°. Spray a 3-inch-deep casserole dish with nonstick cooking spray. Heat oil in a heavy skillet and brown onion, garlic and lamb. Drain off excess juices. Add tomato sauce and seasonings. Let simmer while making white sauce.

Melt butter in a saucepan and whisk in flour. Add milk and cook until thickened. Remove from heat and stir in eggs, Parmesan and nutmeg.

Place ½ of the cooked pasta in casserole and cover with lamb and tomato mixture; top with remaining pasta. Pour white sauce over and sprinkle with cheese. Sprinkle top with additional nutmeg. (Can be refrigerated at this point.) Bake for 1 hour or until puffed and golden.

CHUTNEY CHICKEN

Servings: 6-8

Serve a spinach salad with a sweet and sour dressing and a rice pilaf to compliment this dish.

4 whole chicken breasts, halved
1 tsp. salt
½ tsp. pepper
1½ cups orange juice
½ cup raisins
½ cup chutney
½ tsp. dried thyme
2 tsp. cinnamon
½ tsp. curry powder
½ cup toasted slivered almonds

Heat oven to 350°. Spray a 9-x-13-inch casserole dish with nonstick cooking spray. Cut chicken breasts in half. Place chicken in a single layer in casserole. Combine orange juice, raisins, chutney and spices. Pour over chicken. Bake for 1 hour, basting occasionally. Just before serving, sprinkle with almonds.

REUBEN CASSEROLE

We've loaded all the flavor of a Reuben sandwich into a casserole. To reduce calories, you can substitute Alpine lace low-fat Swiss cheese for regular Swiss cheese.

1 can (27 oz.) sauerkraut, well drained
3 tomatoes, sliced
1/2 cup Thousand Island dressing, regular or reduced-fat
1 lb. thinly sliced deli corned beef
1/2 lb. Swiss or low-fat Alpine Lace cheese, sliced
1 can (8 oz.) Hungry Jack brand biscuits
1/2 tsp. caraway seeds

Heat oven to 425°. Spread sauerkraut in the bottom of a 3-quart casserole. Top with tomato slices and spread each slice with dressing. Layer with corned beef and cheese. Bake for 30 minutes. Open biscuits and separate each one into 3 layers. Arrange over top of casserole and sprinkle with caraway seeds. Continue baking for 10 to 15 more minutes.

INTERNATIONAL FAVORITES   65

GERMAN PORK AND SAUERKRAUT CASSEROLE

Serve with a crusty black bread to soak up the juices.

1½ lb. boneless pork roast, cut into ¾-inch cubes
1 tsp. salt
½ tsp. pepper
½ tsp. garlic powder
2 onions, chopped
1 jar (16 oz.) sauerkraut
1 jar (16 oz.) sweet and sour red cabbage
2 apples, peeled, cored and thinly sliced
½ cup golden raisins
3 tbs. brown sugar

Heat oven to 325°. Combine all ingredients in a heavy 4-quart Dutch oven with a tight-fitting lid. On the stovetop, bring to a simmer over medium heat. Transfer to oven and bake for 2½ to 3 hours or until meat is very tender.

IRISH BEEF AND CABBAGE BAKE

Even those who do not care for cabbage seem to go for this dish.

1 lb. lean ground beef
½ cup chopped onion
1 cup chopped celery
1 can (20 oz.) whole tomatoes and juice
2 tsp. salt
½ tsp. pepper
4 cups chopped cabbage
1 cup soft breadcrumbs
2 tbs. butter or margarine, melted

Heat oven to 375°. Spray a 2½-quart casserole with nonstick cooking spray. Brown beef and onion in a large skillet over medium high-heat, until meat is cooked and onions are tender. Drain off any excess liquid. Add celery, tomatoes, salt and pepper and simmer for 5 minutes, breaking up tomatoes with a spoon. Make alternating layers of cabbage and beef mixture in casserole. Top with crumbs and drizzle with melted butter. Bake for 45 minutes.

SALSA COUSCOUS CHICKEN

Servings: 4

This easy-to-assemble casserole is loaded with flavor and texture. Couscous is a popular Middle Eastern grain (granular semolina), used much like rice.

3 cups hot cooked couscous, prepared
   according to package instructions
1 tbs. vegetable oil
1/2 cup slivered almonds
1 tsp. chopped fresh garlic
8 chicken thighs, skin removed

1 cup salsa
1/4 cup water
1/4 cup raisins
1 tbs. honey
1 tsp. ground cumin
1/2 tsp. cinnamon

Heat oven to 350°. Heat oil in a large skillet over medium-high heat. Stir-cook almonds until brown, remove and set aside.

Add garlic and chicken and cook until browned, turning once, about 4 to 5 minutes. In a bowl, combine salsa, water, raisins, honey and spices. Place cooked couscous in a greased casserole. Top with cooked chicken and pour sauce over. Sprinkle the top with almonds. Bake for 20 minutes.

MEXICAN CASSEROLE

This recipe can easily be doubled to feed a crowd. It makes a nice lunch or brunch dish.

½ lb. pork sausage
½ lb. lean ground beef
1 clove garlic, minced
1 onion, chopped
1 can (4 oz.) whole green chiles
2 cups shredded sharp cheddar
   cheese, regular or low-fat

4 eggs, or egg substitute
¼ cup flour
1½ cups milk, whole or 2%
1 tsp. salt
¼ tsp. Tabasco Sauce

Heat oven to 350°. Spray a 1½-quart casserole with nonstick cooking spray. In a large skillet over medium-high heat, brown pork, beef, garlic and onion until meat is cooked and onion is soft. Drain off any excess liquid. Remove stems and seeds from chiles. Layer ½ of the chiles on the bottom of casserole dish. Top with ½ of the cheese, all of the cooked meat mixture and remaining chiles. In a small bowl, combine eggs, flour, milk, salt and Tabasco. Pour over casserole and sprinkle with remaining cheese. Bake for 45 minutes or until set.

EASY ENCHILADAS

Servings: 4-6

It is much faster just to tear the tortillas into strips and layer them in this quick-to-fix casserole.

1 lb. lean ground beef or turkey
1 onion, chopped
2 cloves garlic, minced
2 cans (10 oz. each) enchilada sauce
1 can (4 oz.) sliced ripe olives
12 oz. cheddar cheese, shredded, regular or
   low-fat
1 tsp. salt
$\frac{1}{2}$ tsp. pepper
12 corn tortillas, torn into strips
sour cream and salsa for serving

Heat oven to 350°. Spray a 2-quart casserole dish with nonstick cooking spray. In a large skillet over medium-high heat, cook ground beef, onion and garlic until tender. Drain off any liquid. Add enchilada sauce, olives, salt and pepper. Place $\frac{1}{2}$ of the tortilla strips in the bottom, add $\frac{1}{2}$ of the meat mixture and $\frac{1}{2}$ of the cheese. Repeat, ending with cheese. Bake for 1 hour. Serve with sour cream and salsa.

SOUR CREAM ENCHILADAS

You can add diced cooked chicken to this recipe if you wish—use about 2 cups. We enjoyed a calorie-packed version of this recipe for years; however, we can now enjoy it more often by substituting low-fat soup, low-fat cheddar, and a low-fat sour cream as we have done in the recipe below.

1 pkg. (about 12 oz.) corn tortillas
2 cans (10¾ oz. each) cream of chicken soup, regular or reduced-fat
1 can (4 oz.) diced green chiles
1 medium onion, chopped
1 pt. sour cream, regular or low-fat
6 green onions, thinly sliced
8 oz. cheddar cheese, shredded, regular or low-fat

Heat oven to 350°. Spray a 1½-quart shallow casserole with nonstick cooking spray. Tear tortillas into 2-inch strips. In a large mixing bowl, combine soup, chiles, onion, sour cream and green onions. Add tortilla strips and mix well. Pour ½ of this mixture into casserole, sprinkle with ½ of the cheese and repeat, ending with cheese. Bake for 45 minutes.

NACHOS CASSEROLE

This makes a good family dinner that kids enjoy. This mixture can also be served with soft flour tortillas

1 1/2 lb. ground beef
2 cups diced green bell peppers
1 onion, chopped
2 tsp. freshly chopped garlic
1 can (15 oz.) red kidney beans, rinsed and drained
1 can (14.5 oz.) diced tomatoes
1 pkg. taco seasoning
1 cup shredded cheddar cheese, regular or low-fat
1 cup sour cream, optional
tortilla chips for serving

Heat oven to 350°. In a large skilled over medium-high heat, cook beef until rumbly. Drain off fat. Stir in peppers and onion and cook until soft. Add garlic, beans, tomatoes and taco seasoning. Pour mixture into a casserole that has been sprayed with nonstick cooking spray. Bake for 20 minutes. Top with cheese and continue baking until cheese melts. Remove from oven and top with sour cream, if desired. Serve with tortilla chips.

CHICKEN AND CHILES MEXICAN-STYLE

Servings: 6

This casserole has a delicious sauce. Serve it with Mexican-style rice.

3 whole chicken breasts, skinned and boned
2 tbs. vegetable oil
1 tsp. salt
1/2 tsp. pepper
1 large white onion, cut lengthwise into strips

2 cans (4 oz. each) diced green chiles
1/3 cup milk, whole or 2%
1 cup sour cream, regular or low-fat
1 large can (7 oz.) whole green chiles
4 oz. cheddar cheese, shredded, regular or low-fat

Heat oven to 350°. Spray a 1 1/2- to 2-quart casserole with nonstick cooking spray. Cut each breasts into 1/2-inch strips. Heat oil in a large nonstick skillet. Cook chicken strips over medium-high heat until done, and sprinkle with salt and pepper. Remove from skillet and set aside. Add onion to skillet and cook until soft. With a food processor or blender, process diced chiles, milk and sour cream until blended. Arrange chicken strips in casserole and top with onion. Cut whole chiles into 1/2-inch strips and place on top. Pour sour cream mixture over and top with cheese. Bake for 20 to 30 minutes or until bubbly.

TAMALE PIE

Servings: 8

Make the filling for this pie the day before and refrigerate overnight for the flavors to mellow. The next day, top with a packaged corn muffin mix batter.

1 large onion, chopped
2 cloves garlic, minced
2 lb. lean ground beef
1 can (8 oz.) tomato sauce
1 pkg. (10 oz.) frozen corn, thawed
1 tbs. chili powder
1 tsp. salt
1/2 tsp. pepper
1 can (4 oz.) diced green chiles, drained
1 can (15 oz.) chili con carne with beans
1 pkg. (16 oz.) corn muffin mix
2 eggs (can be egg substitute)
2/3 cup milk, whole or 2%
1 tsp. dried dill
1 tsp. ground cumin

Heat oven to 400°. Spray a 3-quart casserole with nonstick cooking spray. In a large skillet over medium-high heat, cook beef, onion and garlic until beef is no longer pink and onion is soft. Drain off any excess liquid. Add tomato sauce, corn, chili powder, salt and pepper. Simmer for 10 minutes. Add green chiles and chili con carne. Spoon mixture into casserole. (Can be refrigerated overnight at this point.) Combine corn muffin mix with eggs, milk and seasonings. Pour over meat mixture and bake for 10 minutes. Turn oven to 350° and continue to bake for 30 minutes or until cornbread is done and top is golden.

MEXICALI CASSEROLE

Servings: 6-8

This casserole is a favorite with kids. Garnish with additional shredded cheese, crisp shredded lettuce, salsa, chopped onion and jalapeños.

1 lb. lean ground beef
1 onion, chopped
1 clove garlic, minced
1 can (15 oz.) tomato sauce
1/2 cup water
2 tbs. chili powder
1/2 tsp. dried oregano

1/4 tsp. ground cumin
1 can (16 oz.) red kidney beans, rinsed and drained
1 bag (8 oz.) corn chips
1/2 cup shredded cheddar cheese, regular or low-fat

Heat oven to 350°. Spray a 3-quart casserole with nonstick cooking spray. In a large skillet over medium-high heat, brown beef with onion and garlic. Drain off any excess juices. Add tomato sauce, water and seasonings. In casserole, make alternate layers of meat sauce, beans and corn chips. Cover and bake for 30 minutes. Top with cheese and bake for an additional 10 minutes. Serve with garnishes.

CHEESE AND CHILE BAKE

This can be cut into small squares for an appetizer or served in larger portions with a green salad for a meatless entrée.

$1/2$ lb. Monterey Jack cheese, shredded, regular or low-fat
$1/2$ lb. medium cheddar cheese, shredded, regular or low-fat
2 cans (4 oz. each) diced green chiles
2 eggs, beaten
2 cups milk, whole or 2%
$1/2$ cup flour
1 tsp. salt
$1/2$ tsp. white pepper

Heat oven to 375°. Spray a 9-inch square casserole with nonstick cooking spray. Layer $1/2$ of each of the cheeses and sprinkle with 1 can green chiles. Repeat. In a bowl, combine eggs, milk, flour, salt and pepper. Pour over cheeses and bake for 45 minutes.

CORNMEAL CHILE BAKE

Serve this unusual side dish with a Mexican dinner.

2 cups yellow cornmeal
1 cup milk, whole or 2%
4 eggs
2 tsp. baking powder
1 tsp. salt
2 pkg. (10 oz. each) frozen corn, thawed
2 cups diced red bell pepper
1 can (4 oz.) diced green chiles
2 cups shredded cheddar cheese, regular or low-fat
sour cream, black olives and sliced green onions for
   garnish

Heat oven to 350°. Spray a 9-x-13-inch casserole with nonstick cooking spray. In a bowl combine cornmeal, milk, eggs, baking powder and salt until smooth. Stir in remaining ingredients. Pour into casserole and bake for 40 minutes. Cool and cut into squares. Garnish with sour cream, black olives and sliced green onions.

BAKED CHILES RELLENOS

This recipe makes a tasty luncheon or Sunday night supper, and it's also good as a side dish with grilled foods.

2 cans (7 oz. each) whole green chiles, seeded
1/2 lb. cheddar cheese, shredded, regular or low-fat
1/2 lb. Monterey Jack cheese, shredded, regular or low-fat
2 cups evaporated milk
4 eggs or egg substitute
1/3 cup flour
1 tsp. salt

Heat oven to 350°. Spray an 8-x-12-inch casserole with nonstick cooking spray. Layer chiles and cheeses in the bottom. In a blender or food processor, combine evaporated milk, eggs, flour and salt. Pour over the top. Bake for 45 minutes or until puffed and golden. Cut in squares to serve.

ITALIAN CHICKEN AND VEGETABLE BAKE

Servings: 6

Add a green salad and French bread and your dinner is done. Feel free to add or delete vegetables according to personal taste.

3 whole chicken breasts, halved and skinned
6 large carrots, peeled and cut into 1-inch chunks
6 red potatoes, cut in half
salt and pepper to taste
1 bottle (16 oz.) zesty Italian salad dressing, regular or fat-free
1 cup broccoli florets
1 cup cauliflower florets
1 medium onion, chopped
1 green bell pepper, cut into 1-inch chunks
1 cup sliced fresh mushrooms
1 cup sliced zucchini

Heat oven to 375°. Spray a 3-quart casserole with nonstick cooking spray. Arrange chicken, meat side down, in a single layer in casserole. Cover with carrots and potatoes. Sprinkle with salt and pepper and pour dressing over all. Cover with a lid or foil and bake for 40 minutes. Remove from oven, turn chicken and add broccoli, cauliflower, and onions. Cover again and bake for 20 minutes longer. Add bell pepper, mushrooms and zucchini, and continue to bake for 10 to 15 minutes or until mushrooms are tender.

CHICKEN CACCIATORE

Servings: 4

Serve this Italian favorite with spaghetti or other pasta.

3 lb. chicken pieces of choice
1/2 cup flour
1 tsp. salt
1/2 tsp. pepper
1/2 tsp. dried oregano
1/4 cup vegetable oil
2 medium onions, thinly sliced

2 cloves garlic, minced
1 green bell pepper, chopped
1 cup sliced fresh mushrooms
1 can (8 oz.) tomato sauce
1 can (16 oz.) whole tomatoes with juice

Heat oven to 350°. Spray a 3-quart casserole with nonstick cooking spray. Combine flour and seasonings in a plastic bag, add chicken pieces and shake until coated. Heat oil in a large skillet over medium heat and brown chicken for 5 minutes on each side. Remove chicken from skillet and place in a single layer in casserole. Add onions and garlic to skillet and cook until soft. Add green pepper, mushrooms, tomato sauce and tomatoes to skillet and cook until pepper is tender. Pour over chicken. Cover casserole with a lid and bake for 40 minutes or until chicken is tender.

SPEEDY SPAGHETTI BAKE

Layers of noodles, sauce and cheese make this quick-to-fix casserole. Excellent for carbo-loading.

4 cups prepared spaghetti sauce
1 lb. spaghetti, linguini or angel hair pasta, cooked and drained
1 lb. part skim ricotta cheese or low fat cottage cheese
1 lb. mozzarella cheese, shredded, regular or part skim
4 oz. grated Parmesan cheese

Heat oven to 350°. Spray a 3-quart casserole with nonstick cooking spray. Layer ½ of the cooked noodles in casserole, followed by ½ of the sauce, all of the ricotta and ½ of the mozzarella. Repeat with remaining noodles, sauce and mozzarella. Top with Parmesan. Bake for 30 to 45 minutes or until bubbly and cheeses are melted.

STUFFED PEPPERS ITALIAN-STYLE

This tasty dish makes a beautiful presentation when a variety of red, yellow and green bell peppers are used.

8 red bell peppers
1 1/2 lb. lean ground beef
1/2 lb. ground pork or bulk sausage
1/2 cup cracker crumbs
1 cup grated Romano cheese
2 eggs, well beaten
1/3 cup pine nuts
1/2 cup chopped black olives

1 small onion, chopped
1 clove garlic, minced
1 1/2 tsp. salt
1/2 tsp. crumbled dried oregano
1/4 tsp. pepper
1/2 cup water
grated Romano cheese for garnish

Heat oven to 350°. With nonstick cooking spray, spray a casserole large enough to hold peppers. Slice tops from peppers and remove seeds. Combine remaining ingredients, blend well, and stuff peppers. Place in casserole, add water to dish, cover tightly with lid or foil and bake for 45 minutes or until cooked. Sprinkle with Romano cheese and serve.

PIZZA POPOVER

This dinner is really fun for kids. Use your favorite pizza toppings along with the basic recipe to create your own favorites.

½ lb. ground pork sausage
½ lb. lean ground beef
1 can (15 oz.) tomato sauce
1 cup plus 2 tbs. flour
1 tsp. dried oregano
¼ tsp. salt
12 oz. mozzarella cheese, sliced,
   regular or part skim

2 eggs
1 tbs. corn oil
1 cup milk, whole or 2%
¼ tsp. salt
¼ cup grated Parmesan cheese

Heat oven to 425°. In a large skillet over medium-high heat, cook sausage and beef until crumbly. Drain off fat. Add tomato sauce, 2 tbs. of the flour, oregano and salt. Heat to boiling and cook for 2 minutes. Pour into an ungreased 9-x-13-inch casserole. Arrange cheese slices over top. Beat together eggs, oil, milk, salt and 1 cup flour and pour over cheese and meat. Sprinkle with Parmesan and bake until puffy and cheese has melted, about 25 to 30 minutes. Cut into squares to serve.

TURKEY LASAGNA

Servings: 6-8

This casserole is easy to make, and a great use for leftover turkey.

8 oz. lasagna noodles
1 can (10½ oz.) cream of chicken soup
1 can (10½ oz.) cream of mushroom soup
1 cup shredded Parmesan cheese
1 cup sour cream
1 cup sliced green onions
1 cup sliced black olives
½ cup chopped red bell pepper
1 tsp. chopped garlic
3 cups chopped cooked turkey
2 cups mild cheddar cheese, shredded

Heat oven to 350°. Cook and drain lasagna noodles. Combine remaining ingredients except cheddar. Spray a 9-x-13-inch baking dish with nonstick cooking spray. Place ¼ of the soup mixture on the bottom and top with ⅓ of the noodles. Repeat layers ending with soup mixture. Sprinkle top with cheddar cheese. Bake for 45 minutes.

BAKED CHICKEN KIEV

True chicken Kiev is a boneless chicken breast filled with an herbed butter mixture, rolled in crumbs and deep fried. It is a messy and time-consuming recipe. We think you will find this recipe gives just as much flavor without the work or extra calories of deep frying.

1/2 cup fine dry breadcrumbs
2 tbs. grated Parmesan cheese
1 tsp. chopped fresh basil
1 tsp. dried oregano
1/2 tsp. salt
2 cloves garlic, minced

2 whole chicken breasts, split
2/3 cup butter, melted or margarine
1/4 cup white wine
1/4 cup chopped green onion
1/4 cup chopped fresh parsley

Heat oven to 375°. Spray a 1 1/2-quart casserole with nonstick cooking spray. Combine breadcrumbs, cheese, seasonings and garlic. Dip chicken pieces in melted butter and roll in breadcrumb mixture. Place skin-side up in casserole and bake for 50 minutes. To remaining butter, add wine, green onion and parsley. Drizzle over baked chicken and continue baking for 5 minutes.

INTERNATIONAL FAVORITES   87

SIDE DISHES AND VEGETABLES

SPINACH AND ARTICHOKE CASSEROLE

This is a delicious side dish to serve with poultry, pork or fish. One time we went to the trouble of using chopped fresh spinach and found that we much prefer the frozen, not only for the convenience but also for the end result.

2 jars (6 oz. each) marinated artichoke hearts, drained
2 pkg. (10 oz. each) frozen chopped spinach, thawed
1 pkg. (8 oz.) cream cheese or Neufchatel cheese, softened
2 tbs. butter or margarine
$\frac{1}{2}$ cup shredded Parmesan cheese
paprika

Heat oven to 375°. Spray a shallow 1½-quart casserole with nonstick cooking spray. Arrange drained artichokes in casserole. Place thawed spinach in a clean dishtowel and wring out excess moisture. Layer spinach over artichokes. Combine cream cheese, butter and ½ of the Parmesan cheese in a small bowl or with a food processor. Spread in an even layer over spinach. Sprinkle with remaining Parmesan and paprika. Bake for 30 minutes or until heated through and top is bubbly.

SPINACH SQUARES

Servings: 6-8

These freeze well and can be microwaved without thawing. They make a great hors d'oeuvre, vegetable side dish or accompaniment to soup.

2 bunches green onions, thinly sliced
2 tbs. butter or margarine
1 pkg. (10 oz.) frozen chopped spinach, thawed
1/4 cup minced fresh parsley
1 tsp. seasoning salt
1/2 tsp. pepper
6 eggs or egg substitute
1/4 cup sour cream, regular or low-fat
1/2 cup soft breadcrumbs
3/4 cup shredded Swiss or low-fat Alpine Lace cheese
3/4 cup grated Parmesan cheese
paprika

Heat oven to 350°. Spray a shallow 2-quart casserole with nonstick cooking spray. In a large skillet over medium-high heat, cook green onions until limp. Squeeze spinach in a dishtowel to remove all liquid. Add to pan and cook for 1 minute. In a large bowl, combine onion-spinach mixture with remaining ingredients, except ¼ cup of the Parmesan. Mix well. Pour mixture into casserole and smooth top with a spatula. Sprinkle with remaining Parmesan and paprika. Bake for 20 minutes or until a knife inserted in the center comes out clean. Cut into small squares to serve as an hors d'oeuvre or in larger squares to serve as a vegetable.

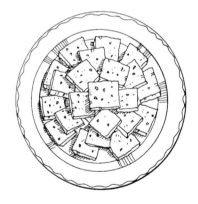

CORN PUDDING

This colorful and easy side dish is always a hit.

1 1/2 cups whole kernel frozen corn, thawed
2 tbs. flour
2 tbs. sugar
2 tbs. butter or margarine
1 tsp. salt
2 eggs
1 small jar (4 oz.) chopped pimientos, drained
1/2 cup chopped green bell pepper
1 cup shredded cheddar cheese
1/2 cup milk, whole or 2%

Heat oven to 350°. Spray a 1-quart casserole with nonstick cooking spray. Mix all ingredients together well. Pour mixture into prepared casserole. Bake for 30 minutes.

CORN AND ZUCCHINI MEXICAN-STYLE

This casserole has a nice combination of colors and flavors.

2 tbs. butter or margarine
1 large onion, chopped
2 lb. zucchini, sliced
2 pkg. (10 oz. each) frozen whole kernel corn
8 oz. Old English processed cheese, cubed
1 can (4 oz.) diced green chiles
1/2 tsp. salt
1/4 tsp. pepper

Heat oven to 350°. Spray a 2-quart casserole with nonstick cooking spray. Melt butter in a large skillet over medium-high heat and cook onion and zucchini until soft. Add remaining ingredients and stir over low heat until cheese is melted. Pour into casserole. Bake uncovered for 30 minutes.

TOMATO PUDDING

This unusual side dish goes well with beef. Try it for something different.

4 cups tomato puree
1/2 tsp. salt
1/8 tsp. pepper
1 cup brown sugar, packed
4 cups cubed bread, crusts removed
1/3 cup butter, melted or margarine

Heat oven to 350°. Spray a 1 1/2-quart casserole dish with nonstick cooking spray. Combine tomato puree, salt, pepper and sugar in a saucepan and bring to a boil. Place bread cubes in casserole. Pour melted butter over bread and toss to coat. Pour hot tomato mixture over bread. Bake for 45 minutes.

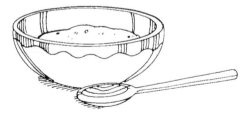

MUSHROOM BAKE

This dish makes a wonderful accompaniment to roast beef.

½ cup butter or margarine
1½ lb. fresh mushrooms, sliced
1 onion, finely chopped
2 tbs. flour
1 cup sour cream, regular or low-fat
¼ cup whipping cream or evaporated
  skim milk

1 tsp. salt
½ tsp. pepper
¼ tsp. nutmeg
2 tbs. chopped fresh parsley
¼ cup breadcrumbs
2 tbs. butter or margarine, melted

Heat oven to 325°. Spray a 1½-quart casserole with nonstick cooking spray. Melt butter in a large skillet over medium-high heat. Add mushrooms and cook until beginning to brown. Add onion and cook until soft. Stir in flour and cook until thick. Add sour cream, whipping cream and seasonings. Pour into casserole, top with crumbs and drizzle with melted butter. Bake for 35 minutes or until golden brown and bubbly.

MUSHROOM STRATA

This dish works well as a main course or side dish.

2 tbs. butter or margarine
1 lb. fresh mushrooms, sliced
$1/2$ cup chopped onion
$1/2$ cup chopped celery
$1/2$ cup chopped green bell pepper
1 tsp. salt
$1/2$ tsp. pepper
$1/2$ cup mayonnaise, regular or low-fat
6 slices firm white bread, crusts removed
2 tbs. butter
2 eggs, beaten or egg substitute
$1 1/2$ cups milk, whole or 2%
1 cup shredded cheddar cheese, regular or low-fat

Spray a 9-inch casserole with nonstick cooking spray. Melt butter in a large skillet over medium-high heat and cook mushrooms, onion, celery and green pepper until soft. Sprinkle with salt and pepper and let cool. Add mayonnaise. Spread bread with 2 tbs. butter and cut into cubes. Place 1/2 of the bread cubes in casserole and spread with mushroom mixture. Top with remaining bread cubes. Beat eggs and milk together and pour over top. Cover and refrigerate overnight.

Heat oven to 325°. Bake casserole for 45 minutes, top with cheese and continue baking for 15 minutes longer. Cut into squares to serve.

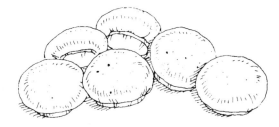

GREEN TOMATO CASSEROLE

Here's a great way to use up the last green tomatoes before the first frost. This surprising combination of ingredients is absolutely delicious.

¹/₄ cup butter or margarine
8 large green tomatoes, cut into
    ¹/₂-inch slices
2 large onions, thinly sliced and
    separated into rings
1 tsp. sugar
1 tsp. curry powder

1 tsp. paprika
1 tsp. salt
2 cups sour cream, regular or low-fat
¹/₂ cup milk, whole or 2%
¹/₄ cup breadcrumbs
¹/₂ cup grated Parmesan cheese

Heat oven to 350°. Spray a 2-quart casserole with nonstick cooking spray. In a large skillet over medium-high heat, melt butter and cook green tomato slices in batches until tender, turning once. Layer tomatoes and onion slices in casserole, sprinkling with sugar and seasonings. In a bowl, combine sour cream and milk. Pour over top of casserole. Sprinkle top with breadcrumbs and cheese. Bake for 20 to 30 minutes or until sour cream begins to bubble. Do not overbake or sour cream will curdle.

BROCCOLI AND SPINACH BAKE

Servings: 8

Great to serve for a buffet side dish. Cook broccoli and spinach according to package directions. Line a strainer with a clean dish towel, and after the vegetables have cooled, wring them in the towel to remove excess moisture.

2 pkg. (10 oz.) frozen chopped broccoli
2 pkg. (10 oz.) frozen chopped spinach
1 pt. sour cream, regular or low-fat
1 pkg. dry onion soup mix
3/4 cup shredded cheddar cheese, regular or low-fat

Heat oven to 325°. Spray a shallow 2-quart casserole with nonstick cooking spray. Cook vegetables until broccoli is tender-crisp and drain well. In a bowl, combine sour cream and onion soup mix. Add vegetables and combine. Pour into casserole and sprinkle with cheddar. Bake for 30 minutes.

STUFFING SOUFFLÉ

Here's something new to do with zucchini. Serve it as a side dish or brunch entrée.

1 cup Stove Top Stuffing crumbs
2½ tbs. flour
1 cup sliced mushrooms
⅓ cup thinly sliced sweet onion
⅓ cup thinly sliced green bell pepper
1 medium zucchini, thinly sliced
1 cup shredded Swiss or low-fat Alpine Lace cheese
6 eggs or egg substitute
2½ cups milk, whole or 2%

Heat oven to 350°. Spray a 2-quart casserole dish with nonstick cooking spray. Spread stuffing crumbs in casserole and sprinkle evenly with flour. Top with mushrooms, onion, pepper and zucchini. Sprinkle with cheese. In a medium bowl, beat eggs, 1 tsp. of the seasoning packet mixture and milk. Pour over top of cheese and vegetables. Bake for 60 minutes or until eggs are set and a toothpick inserted in the middle comes out clean. Let stand for 10 minutes before serving.

CAULIFLOWER CUSTARD

Here's something different to serve for a side dish.

2 pkg. (10 oz. each) frozen cauliflower, cooked and drained
2 eggs or egg substitute, beaten
3/4 cup milk, whole or 2%
4 oz. cheddar cheese, regular or low-fat,
   shredded
3 tbs. chopped fresh parsley
3 tbs. butter or margarine, melted
1 tbs. minced onion
1/2 tsp. salt
1/4 tsp. pepper
1/2 cup breadcrumbs
2 tbs. butter or margarine, melted

Heat oven to 350°. Spray a 1-quart casserole with nonstick cooking spray. Place cauliflower in casserole. In a bowl, combine eggs, milk, cheddar, parsley, butter and seasonings. Pour over cauliflower. Top with crumbs and drizzle with melted butter. Bake for 30 minutes.

LAYERED ZUCCHINI CASSEROLE

Servings: 6

This versatile, colorful and healthy casserole has a lot going for it. It goes well with chicken, beef, barbecues and Italian food. You can adjust the cooking temperature and time in order to go with other foods in your oven. You can serve this dish tender-crisp or soft and juicy, depending on your personal preference. You can vary the seasonings or leave it natural. This is a healthy vegetarian recipe that even kids enjoy. The beauty of this casserole is you can experiment as you wish.

2 zucchini, unpeeled
1 onion
1 green bell pepper
2 tomatoes

seasonings: salt, pepper, garlic,
    oregano, basil or parsley, optional
6 oz. sharp cheddar cheese, regular or
    low-fat, shredded

Heat oven to chosen temperature. Spray a 2-quart casserole with nonstick cooking spray. Trim zucchini ends flat and cut zucchini into 1/4-inch slices. Arrange zucchini slices in casserole. Cut onion into very thin slices. Separate into rings and layer on top of zucchini. Slice green pepper and tomatoes and layer on top of onions. Sprinkle with seasonings to taste, if using. Top with cheese. Bake, uncovered, at 300° for 1 1/2 hours, at 350° for 1 hour or at 400° for 45 minutes.

SQUASH CASSEROLE WITH SMOKED GOUDA

Servings: 6

To speed preparation of this dish, use salad spinach that comes already washed in the produce section of the grocery store.

8 oz. yellow squash, cut into $1/2$-inch slices
8 oz. zucchini, cut into $1/2$-inch slices
2 medium onions, chopped
1 lb. fresh spinach, coarsely chopped
1 lb. smoked Gouda cheese, grated
1 tsp. chopped garlic
1 tbs. chopped fresh thyme
1 tsp. seasoning salt
$1/2$ tsp. pepper
1 cup half-and-half
1 cup breadcrumbs

Heat oven to 350°. In a large bowl, stir together squash, onion, spinach, cheese and seasonings. Place in a shallow greased casserole. Pour half-and-half over top and sprinkle with breadcrumbs. Bake for 25 minutes or until squash is tender.

SWEET ONION CASSEROLE

Servings: 6-8

Use a mild sweet onion, such as Vidalia or Walla Walla Sweet, to make this unusual side dish.

3 cups thinly sliced onions
1/4 cup butter or margarine
1 cup grated sharp cheddar cheese, regular or low-fat
3 eggs or egg substitute
1 cup milk, whole or 2%
1/4 tsp. dried thyme

1/2 tsp. salt
1/4 tsp. pepper
1/2 cup crushed cheese crackers
8 slices bacon, cooked crisp and crumbled
1 tbs. poppy seeds

Heat oven to 350°. Spray a 2-quart casserole with nonstick cooking spray. In a large skillet over medium-high heat, cook onions in butter until tender. Place onions in bottom. Sprinkle with cheese. In a mixing bowl, beat together eggs, milk and seasonings. Pour over onions. Sprinkle with cracker crumbs, bacon and poppy seeds. Bake uncovered for 30 minutes, until golden.

BAKED RATATOUILLE

This tasty vegetable casserole originated in France.

2 medium onions, sliced
6 cloves garlic, minced
1/2 cup olive oil
1 large eggplant, quartered and cut into 1/2-inch
    slices
3 zucchini, sliced
1 can (16 oz.) stewed tomatoes
2 green bell peppers, cored and sliced into
    rounds
1 tsp. salt
1/2 tsp. pepper

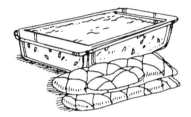

Heat oven to 350°. Spray a 3-inch-deep casserole with nonstick cooking spray. In large skillet, cook onions and garlic in olive oil until tender. Layer eggplant, zucchini, tomatoes, green peppers and onion mixture in casserole, making 3 layers. Bake for 45 minutes. Serve hot or cold.

SWEET POTATOES WITH PECAN TOPPING

Servings: 10-12

These delightful sweet potatoes are accented with orange juice and have a crunchy sweet topping. It's a great dish for the holidays.

2 cans (2 lb. 8 oz. each) sweet
   potatoes or yams, drained
1/3 cup orange juice
1 tbs. grated orange zest
5 tbs. brandy
2 tsp. salt

1/2 tsp. pepper
1 tsp. ground ginger
1/4 cup butter or margarine, melted
1/3 cup brown sugar, packed
2 eggs
Pecan Topping, recipe follows

Heat oven to 350°. Spray a 2-quart casserole with nonstick cooking spray. Combine all ingredients with an electric mixer until light and fluffy. Pour sweet potatoes into the casserole, smooth top and sprinkle with *Pecan Topping*. Bake casserole for 45 minutes.

PECAN TOPPING

2/3 cup brown sugar
1/2 cup butter or margarine

1 cup chopped pecans
1 tsp. cinnamon

Combine ingredients in a small bowl.

RICH POTATO CASSEROLE

You can also use frozen shredded hash browns for the recipe to save time.

9 medium potatoes, boiled, peeled and shredded
1 can (10¾ oz.) cream of chicken soup
1 pint sour cream
1 tsp. seasoned salt
½ tsp. white pepper
½ cup thinly sliced green onions
1½ cups shredded cheddar cheese, regular or low-fat
1 cup cornflake crumbs or crushed potato chips
¼ cup butter, melted

Heat oven to 350°. Place potatoes in a large bowl. Combine soup, sour cream, salt and pepper. Stir into potatoes. Add onions and cheese and mix well. Pour into a greased casserole. Top with crumbs and drizzle with butter. Bake for 45 minutes or until potatoes are tender and top is brown and bubbly.

LITHUANIAN POTATOES

This dish is so delicious, you must try to forget about the calories.

8 oz. bacon, diced
1 large onion, chopped
4 large potatoes, peeled and grated
4 eggs, beaten
1 cup milk
1 tbs. chopped fresh parsley
salt and pepper to taste

Heat oven to 375°. In a large skillet, cook bacon until limp. Pour off excess fat and add onion. Continue cooking until bacon is crisp and onion is soft. Place potatoes in a large mixing bowl; add bacon mixture, eggs, milk and seasoning. Pour into a greased casserole. Bake for 1 hour or until top is golden and potatoes are tender.

CRISP POTATO CASSEROLE

Here's another way to dress up mashed potatoes. If you make it ahead, place the French fried onions on top just before baking.

2 cups mashed potatoes
8 oz. cream cheese, room temperature
1 small onion, finely chopped
2 eggs
2 tbs. flour
1 tsp. salt
$\frac{1}{2}$ tsp. white pepper
1 can ($3\frac{1}{2}$ oz.) French fried onions, crumbled

Heat oven to 325°. Using an electric mixer, combine potatoes, cream cheese, onion, eggs, flour, salt and pepper until light and fluffy. Butter a 2-quart casserole. Spoon potato mixture evenly into pan. Sprinkle onions evenly over top. Bake uncovered for 30 minutes.

POTATO AND CARROT BAKE

Servings: 6-8

Yogurt adds tang to this colorful casserole. It goes well with ham or chicken.

6 medium potatoes, peeled and
  shredded
6 carrots, peeled and shredded
1 large onion, chopped
2 cloves garlic, minced
3 cups plain yogurt, or low-fat or nonfat
  yogurt
1/3 cup vegetable oil
2 eggs, beaten

1 tsp. seasoning salt
1 tsp. salt
1/2 tsp. pepper
8 oz. cheddar cheese, regular or low-
  fat, shredded
1 cup sliced almonds, optional
1 tbs. chopped fresh parsley for
  garnish

Heat oven to 350°. Spray a 3-quart casserole with nonstick cooking spray. In a large bowl, combine shredded potatoes and carrots. Chop onion and garlic with a food processor or by hand. Add yogurt, oil, eggs and seasonings and combine. Add mixture to potatoes and stir well. Pour into casserole and top with cheese, and almonds if using. Bake for 1 1/2 hours. Sprinkle with parsley and serve.

COTTAGE CHEESE NOODLE BAKE

Servings: 8

This rich noodle bake is sure to become one of your favorite side dishes. It is possible to cut some of the calories with low-fat sour cream and cottage cheese.

1 pkg. (8 oz.) noodles, cooked and drained
1 cup cottage cheese, regular or low-fat
1 cup sour cream, regular or low-fat
1/2 cup milk, whole or 2%
2 tsp. Worcestershire sauce
1 small onion, finely chopped
1 clove garlic, minced
1 tsp. salt
1/2 tsp. pepper
1 cup breadcrumbs
3 tbs. butter or margarine, melted

Heat oven to 350°. Spray a shallow 2-quart casserole with nonstick cooking spray. Combine all ingredients, except breadcrumbs and butter, in a large bowl. Top with crumbs and drizzle with butter. Bake for 20 to 30 minutes, or until bubbly and top is golden.

BAKED NOODLES WITH OLIVES AND BASIL

Servings: 6

This colorful side dish goes with chicken, beef or lamb. Fresh basil makes all the difference in the world.

1 pkg. (12 oz.) egg noodles, cooked and drained
1 pkg. (8 oz.) cream cheese (can be Neufchatel)
1 can (4 oz.) chopped black olives, drained
1/4 cup butter or margarine
1/2 cup chopped fresh basil
1 tsp. salt
1/2 tsp. pepper
1/2 cup grated Parmesan cheese

Heat oven to 325°. Spray a 2-quart casserole with nonstick cooking spray. Combine hot cooked noodles with cream cheese, olives, butter, basil, salt and pepper. Pour into prepared casserole and top with cheese. Bake for 20 to 30 minutes.

BAKED BARLEY AND MUSHROOMS

This makes an unusual side dish for chicken, pork or beef. For variation, add some toasted slivered almonds or chopped macadamia nuts to the dish.

2 onions, chopped
$1/2$ cup butter or margarine
2 cups barley
1 lb. fresh mushrooms, sliced
5 cups boiling chicken broth
1 tsp. salt
$1/2$ tsp. pepper
$1/4$ cup chopped fresh parsley

Heat oven to 350°. Spray a 2-quart casserole with nonstick cooking spray. In a large skillet over medium-high heat, cook onions in butter until soft. Add barley and cook until nutty brown. Place onions and barley in casserole, add mushrooms and pour boiling broth over top. Season with salt and pepper. Bake barley for 1 to $1 1/2$ hours or until tender. Stir in parsley and serve.

RICE MONTEREY

This is a good side dish to serve with barbecued steaks or burgers.

1 cup uncooked rice
1 1/2 pt. sour cream, regular or low-fat
2 cans (4 oz. each) diced green chiles
1 1/2 tsp. salt
1/2 tsp. white pepper
12 oz. shredded Monterey Jack cheese, regular or low-fat

Heat oven to 350°. Spray a 2-quart casserole with nonstick cooking spray. Cook rice. Mix with remaining ingredients, saving 1/2 cup of cheese for the top. Pour rice mixture into casserole and top with cheese. Bake for 30 to 40 minutes.

MEXICAN RICE WITH BLACK BEANS

Servings: 6-8

Black beans are sometimes called "turtle beans," and are available dry or canned. This makes an unusual accompaniment to a Mexican meal.

1 1/2 cups uncooked white rice
1 can (16 oz.) black beans, rinsed and drained
3 cloves garlic, minced
1 tsp. salt
1/2 tsp. white pepper
1 large red onion, chopped
1/2 lb. ricotta cheese, regular or part skim
1/2 cup milk, whole or 2%
6 oz. Monterey Jack cheese, shredded, regular or low-fat
1 can (4 oz.) diced green chiles

Heat oven to 350°. Spray a 2-quart casserole with nonstick cooking spray. Cook rice until tender. Combine rice and black beans in a large bowl. In a medium bowl, mix remaining ingredients, except 1/3 of the Monterey Jack cheese. Combine ricotta mixture with rice mixture. Pour into casserole and top with remaining cheese. Bake for 30 minutes.

PROVENÇAL EGGPLANT AND RICE

Servings: 6-8

Steaming the vegetables, rather than cooking them in oil, eliminates much of the fat in this casserole. Serve as a vegetarian main dish or a hearty side dish.

1 eggplant, peeled and cut into ½-inch slices
4 zucchini, unpeeled, cut into ½-inch slices
2 tbs. vegetable oil
2 onions, chopped
1 red bell pepper, cut into strips
1 green bell pepper, cut into strips
4 large cloves garlic, minced
2 cans (16 oz. each) stewed tomatoes, drained and coarsely chopped
¼ cup chopped fresh parsley
1 tsp. dried basil
1 tsp. dried thyme
1 tsp. salt
½ tsp. pepper
3 cups cooked rice
¼ cup grated Swiss cheese
¼ cup grated Parmesan cheese

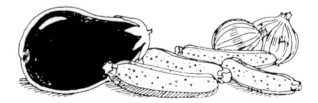

Heat oven to 400°. Spray a 3-quart casserole with nonstick cooking spray. Place eggplant and zucchini on a rimmed baking pan, about 12-x-16 inches, and brush lightly with some of the oil. Cover pan tightly with foil and bake for 20 to 25 minutes or until eggplant is soft. Remove from oven and set aside.

In a large skillet over medium-high heat, combine onions, peppers and garlic with remaining oil and cook until soft. Add tomatoes and seasonings and simmer for 15 minutes. In a large bowl, combine rice with tomato mixture. Place ½ of the rice-tomato mixture in the casserole and cover with eggplant and zucchini. Top with remaining rice-tomato mixture and sprinkle with cheeses. (Can be covered and refrigerated at this point.) Bake for 30 to 35 minutes or until bubbly.

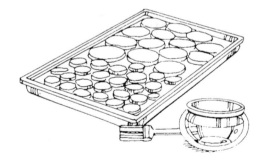

CRAZY BAKED BEANS

The apples add an interesting flavor to this dish.

1 onion, chopped
2 medium apples, peeled, cored and chopped
water to cover
1 can (31 oz.) pork and beans in tomato sauce
6 oz. smoked sausage links, cooked and sliced
³⁄₄ cup raisins, rinsed in hot water
¹⁄₄ cup ketchup
1 tbs. mustard
¹⁄₂ tsp. cinnamon
1 dash cayenne pepper

Heat oven to 375°. In a small saucepan, cook apples and onion in water until tender-crisp. Drain well. Stir all ingredients together and pour into a 1¹⁄₂-quart casserole. Bake for 1 hour and 15 minutes; stir once.

PINEAPPLE CASSEROLE

This side dish is always a favorite holiday indulgence when most folks are ignoring calories! It is particularly good with ham.

$1/2$ cup sugar
3 tbs. flour
3 eggs
1 can (20 oz.) unsweetened crushed pineapple with juice
4 slices white bread, cut into $1/2$-inch cubes
$1/2$ cup butter or margarine, melted

Heat oven to 350°. Butter a 9-inch casserole. In a bowl, combine sugar, flour and eggs. Stir in pineapple and juice. Pour into casserole, top with bread cubes and drizzle with melted butter. Bake for 1 hour.

SOUP-ER EASY

In this chapter you will find some very tasty casseroles that feature soup as part of the sauce. They are a snap to put together and are great for in-a-hurry meals. Low-fat and reduced calorie soups can cut the calories in these dishes substantially.

CHICKEN AND STUFFING CASSEROLE

Servings: 12

You can make this casserole the night before—just omit the dressing until you are ready to bake. This is also a nice way to use up leftover turkey.

4 whole chicken breasts
water to cover
1 dash garlic salt
1 tbs. soy sauce
1 tbs. Worcestershire sauce
2 cans (10¾ oz. each) cream of
  chicken soup, regular or reduced-fat

1 cup milk, regular or 2%
1 cup sour cream, regular or low-fat
1 pkg. (8 oz.) Pepperidge Farm dressing
  mix

In a large saucepan, cover chicken with water, garlic salt, soy sauce and Worcestershire sauce. Bring to a boil, reduce heat and simmer for 20 minutes. Let cool in broth.

Heat oven to 350°. Spray a shallow 3-quart casserole with nonstick cooking spray. Remove skin and bones from chicken and cut into nice large pieces. Arrange chicken pieces in casserole. Combine soup, milk and sour cream. Pour over chicken. (Can be refrigerated overnight at this point.) Sprinkle with dressing mix and bake for 1 hour.

CRUNCHY CHICKEN CASSEROLE

Servings: 4

This tasty casserole is loaded with crunchy vegetables. We do notice the difference when we use the reduced fat products—there is a bit more liquid. However, it is still delicious. Omit the can of onion rings if you are cooking the low fat version. You can pour the Chinese noodles into a pan and bake them while the casserole is cooking for the last 10 minutes and they will be even more crunchy.

2 cups diced cooked chicken or turkey
1 cup sliced celery
1 cup sliced fresh mushrooms
1/4 cup diced red or green bell pepper
2 tbs. finely diced onion
1 can (10³/4 oz.) cream of celery soup, regular or reduced-fat

1/2 cup mayonnaise, regular or reduced-fat
1 can (8 oz.) sliced water chestnuts
1 can (2.8 oz.) French fried onion rings, optional
1 can (4 oz.) Chinese chow mein noodles

Heat oven to 350°. Spray a 1¹/2-quart casserole with nonstick cooking spray. Place chicken and vegetables in a large mixing bowl. Combine soup and mayonnaise and pour over chicken. Add water chestnuts and stir to combine. Pour mixture into casserole. Top with onion rings if desired. Bake for 30 minutes. Place portions of crisp noodles on each plate and spoon casserole over the top.

CHICKEN AND ARTICHOKE CASSEROLE

Servings: 6

This rich-tasting casserole is nice enough for company. Serve with a rice pilaf and a green salad with avocado, red onion and oranges for an excellent combination.

3 lb. chicken breasts or thighs, or combination
1 can (10¾ oz.) cream of mushroom soup, regular or reduced-fat
½ cup sour cream
½ cup dry sherry
1 tbs. minced fresh parsley

1 tsp. dried rosemary
1 tsp. dried thyme
2 cups sliced fresh mushrooms
2 pkg. (10 oz. each) frozen artichoke hearts, thawed
½ cup freshly grated Parmesan cheese
paprika

Heat oven to 350°. Spray a shallow 3-quart casserole with nonstick cooking spray. Arrange chicken pieces in casserole in a single layer. In a bowl, combine soup, sour cream, sherry and seasonings until blended. Stir in mushrooms and artichokes. Pour over chicken. Cover dish with a lid or foil and bake for 1 hour. Sprinkle with Parmesan and paprika and continue baking for 10 minutes.

CHICKEN IN SOUR CREAM SAUCE

Servings: 4-8

Always rinse chicken with cold water after it comes from the package, and blot dry with paper towels. We have added chopped onion and green bell pepper to this recipe, and it was very good too.

8 chicken breast halves
1 can (10¾ oz.) cream of mushroom soup,
   regular or reduced-fat
½ cup sherry
1 cup sour cream, regular or low-fat
1 cup sliced fresh mushrooms
paprika
fresh parsley for garnish

Heat oven to 350°. Spray a shallow 3-quart casserole with nonstick cooking spray. Arrange chicken pieces in casserole. Combine soup, sherry and sour cream. Pour over chicken. Top with mushrooms and sprinkle with paprika. Cover with a lid or foil and bake for 1 hour. Uncover and continue baking for 15 minutes longer. Garnish with parsley.

CHEESE-BAKED CHICKEN

A rich cheese sauce forms as this dish is baking. Use Muenster, Jack or Swiss cheese.

8 boneless, skinless chicken breast halves
8 oz. cheese, cut into slices
1 can (10$\frac{3}{4}$ oz.) cream of chicken soup, regular or reduced-fat
$\frac{1}{4}$ cup dry white wine
2 cups seasoned stuffing mix, crushed
$\frac{1}{3}$ cup butter or margarine, melted
paprika

Heat oven to 350°. Spray a shallow 2-quart casserole with nonstick cooking spray. Arrange chicken breasts in a single layer in dish. Top each piece with a cheese slice. Mix soup with wine and pour over chicken. Sprinkle with crushed stuffing mix and drizzle with butter. Sprinkle with paprika. Bake for 45 to 55 minutes.

EASY CHICKEN DIVAN

This popular casserole has been around for years but still hasn't lost its appeal.

2 pkg. (10 oz. each) frozen chopped broccoli
3 whole chicken breasts
water to cover
1 tbs. soy sauce
1 tbs. Worcestershire sauce
1 tsp. garlic powder
1 can (10¾ oz.) cream of chicken soup, regular or reduced-fat
1 cup mayonnaise
2 tsp. lemon juice
2 cups shredded cheddar cheese, regular or low-fat
1 cup crushed potato chips, optional

Cook broccoli until tender, rinse with cold water to stop the cooking and drain well. In a large pan, cover chicken breasts with water, soy sauce, Worcestershire sauce and garlic. Bring to a boil, reduce heat and simmer until done, about 25 minutes. Drain and cool.

Heat oven to 350°. Spray a 3-quart casserole with nonstick cooking spray. Remove skin and bones from chicken and cut meat into large pieces. Place cooked broccoli in casserole. Top with chicken. Combine soup, mayonnaise and lemon juice and pour over chicken. Sprinkle with cheese, and crushed potato chips if using. Bake for 40 minutes.

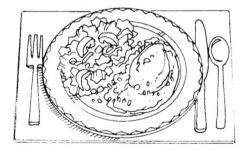

QUICK AND EASY CHICKEN CASSEROLE

Servings: 4-6

This easy-to-assemble dish cooks all by itself. Add a salad and your meal is complete.

1 cup quick cooking rice, such as Minute Rice, uncooked
1 pkg. (1.5 oz.) dry onion soup mix
1 can (10¾ oz.) cream of mushroom soup, regular or reduced-fat
1½ cups water
1 frying chicken, cut into pieces

Heat oven to 350°. Place rice in an ungreased 3-quart casserole. Top with dry soup mix, soup and water. Stir well. Place chicken on top and bake for 30 minutes. Cover casserole with a tight-fitting lid or foil and continue to cook for 1 hour longer.

CRUNCHY TUNA NOODLE CASSEROLE

Most of the ingredients for this casserole can be found on your pantry shelf. Who doesn't need a good old reliable tuna casserole from time to time? The texture in this one makes it particularly appealing.

6 oz. egg noodles, cooked and drained
2 cans (7 oz. each) water-packed tuna, drained
1 cup coarsely chopped celery
$1/3$ cup chopped green bell pepper
$1/3$ cup sliced green onions
1 can (8 oz.) sliced water chestnuts, drained
$1/2$ cup mayonnaise

$1/2$ tsp. dried thyme
$1/4$ tsp. salt
$1/4$ tsp. pepper
1 can (10 oz.) cream of celery soup, regular or reduced-fat
$1/2$ cup milk
$3/4$ cup shredded sharp cheddar cheese, regular or low-fat
$1/4$ cup chopped toasted almonds

Heat oven to 375°. Spray a 2-quart casserole with nonstick cooking spray. Mix all ingredients together, except $1/4$ cup of the cheese, and the almonds. Pour into casserole. Top with cheese and almonds. Bake for 30 minutes, or until browned and bubbly.

CRAB SOUFFLÉ

This is a good way to stretch expensive crabmeat. It makes a nice luncheon dish.

8 slices French bread
2 cups fresh cooked crabmeat
1/2 cup mayonnaise
1 onion, chopped
1 green bell pepper, chopped
1 cup chopped celery
3 cups milk, whole or 2%

4 eggs, beaten, or egg substitute
1 can (10¾ oz.) cream of mushroom
    soup, regular or reduced-fat
1 cup shredded cheddar cheese,
    regular or low-fat
paprika

Heat oven to 325°. Spray a 9-x-9-inch casserole with nonstick cooking spray. Dice 1/2 of the bread and distribute in casserole. Mix crabmeat, mayonnaise, onion, green pepper and celery. Spread over bread cubes. Trim crusts from remaining 4 slices of bread. Place on top of crabmeat. Mix milk, eggs and soup until blended, and pour over top. Bake for 30 minutes, top with cheese and sprinkle with paprika. Continue baking for 30 minutes longer.

OYSTERS AND WILD RICE CASSEROLE

Servings: 8-10

If you like these two exotic foods, you will enjoy this special treat.

1/2 cup butter or margarine, melted
12 oz. wild rice, cooked
1 qt. oysters, drained
1 tsp. salt
1/2 tsp. pepper
1 dash Tabasco Sauce
1 can (10 3/4 oz.) cream of mushroom soup, regular or reduced-fat

1 cup half-and-half or evaporated skim milk
1 1/2 tsp. onion powder
3/4 tsp. dried thyme
1 1/2 tbs. curry powder dissolved in 2 tbs. hot water
1/2 cup finely chopped fresh parsley

Heat oven to 325°. Spray a 3-quart casserole with nonstick cooking spray. Combine melted butter with wild rice and spread 1/2 of the rice in the casserole. Place oysters on top and sprinkle with salt, pepper and Tabasco. Place remaining rice mixture on top. In a small saucepan, combine soup, half-and-half, onion powder, thyme and curry dissolved in hot water. Bring to a boil, stirring constantly. Pour soup mixture over top of casserole. Bake for 45 minutes. Garnish with parsley.

HAM, BROCCOLI AND POTATO SCALLOP

The colors and flavors of this dish are delicious. It's a nice winter supper.

4 medium potatoes, cooked and peeled
1 pkg. (10 oz.) frozen broccoli spears
2 cups cubed ham
1 can (10¾ oz.) cream of mushroom soup, regular or reduced-fat
½ cup milk
1 cup shredded sharp cheddar cheese
1 cup soft breadcrumbs
2 tbs. butter or margarine, melted

Heat oven to 350°. Spray a shallow 1½-quart casserole with nonstick cooking spray. Cut potatoes into ¼-inch-thick slices. Layer ½ of the potato slices in casserole. Cook broccoli until just tender-crisp. Drain well. Layer ½ of the broccoli over potatoes and top with ½ of the ham. Repeat layers. In a small saucepan, combine soup, milk and cheese; heat until smooth. Pour over casserole. Top with crumbs and drizzle with butter. Bake for 45 minutes.

LAZY DAY BEEF STEW

This simple stew can cook all day and just gets better and better—a recipe from good old Mom!

1 tbs. vegetable oil
2 lb. beef stew meat, cut in 1-inch cubes
2 onions, chopped
4 carrots, cut into 1-inch chunks
2 large potatoes, peeled and cut into cubes
2 cans (10 oz. each) tomato soup
1 tsp. salt
1/2 tsp. pepper

Heat oven to 275°. Heat oil in a heavy Dutch oven and brown meat. Drain off any excess juices. Top meat with onions, carrots and potatoes. Pour soup over the top and sprinkle with salt and pepper. Bake for 5 hours.

BEEF AND RICE CASSEROLE

Servings: 6-8

This easy-to-fix entrée freezes well and makes a quick supper on a busy night.

1 1/2 lb. lean ground beef
1 cup chopped onion
2 cloves garlic, minced
8 oz. fresh mushrooms, sliced
1 cup sliced celery
1 pkg. (6 1/4 oz.) Uncle Ben's Long Grain
  and Wild Rice
1 tsp. salt

1/2 tsp. pepper
1 can (10 3/4 oz.) cream of mushroom
  soup, regular or reduced-fat
1 can (10 3/4 oz.) cream of chicken
  soup, regular or reduced-fat
1/2 cup milk
1/2 cup water

Heat oven to 350°. Spray a 3-quart casserole with nonstick cooking spray. In a large skillet over medium-high heat, cook beef, onion, garlic and mushrooms until beef is browned. Drain off any excess liquid. In a large bowl, combine beef mixture with remaining ingredients. Pour into casserole. Bake uncovered for 2 hours.

BAKED LAMB WITH SOUR CREAM WINE SAUCE

If the sauce is too thin for you, mix 2 tsp. of cornstarch with 1 tbs. of water and stir into the mixture 15 minutes before serving. This goes well with noodles or rice.

3½ lb. boneless lamb, cut in 1-inch cubes
2 tbs. vegetable oil
1 cup chopped onion
1 lb. fresh mushrooms, sliced
2 cans (10¾ oz. each) cream of mushroom soup, regular or reduced-fat

1 cup burgundy wine
1 tbs. sugar
1 tsp. salt
1 tsp. crumbled oregano
½ tsp. pepper
1 cup sour cream, regular or low-fat
2 tsp. cornstarch mixed with 1 tbs. water, optional

Heat oven to 325°. In a heavy Dutch oven, cook lamb in oil over medium-high heat until cooked on all sides. Add onion and mushrooms and cook until onions are soft. Add soup, wine and seasonings. Cover with a tight-fitting lid. Bake for 2 hours. Remove from oven and stir in sour cream. Thicken with cornstarch if desired. Continue baking for 15 minutes longer or until heated through and thickened.

BUFFET POTATO BAKE

People go for this rich potato casserole in a BIG way, so be sure to make a lot. It's ideal for entertaining, as it must be made ahead.

1 can (10¾ oz.) cream of chicken soup, regular or reduced-fat
¼ cup butter or margarine
1 pt. sour cream, regular or low-fat
1½ cups shredded cheddar cheese, regular or low-fat
½ cup sliced green onions
1 pkg. (20 oz.) frozen shredded potatoes for hash browns, thawed
 ½ cup cornflake crumbs or crushed potato chips

Heat oven to 350°. Spray a shallow 2-quart casserole with nonstick cooking spray. In a large bowl, combine soup, butter, sour cream, cheese and green onions. Stir in potatoes. Pour into casserole. Top with crumbs and bake for 1 hour or until bubbly and golden.

SUMMER SQUASH CASSEROLE

Here's another wonderful recipe to have on hand when your garden gets over-zealous with the zucchini production. This goes well with pork roast or chicken. The seasoning in the stuffing crumbs complements the casserole nicely.

3 cups unpeeled zucchini or any other summer squash
1/2 pkg. Pepperidge Farm stuffing crumbs
1/3 cup butter or margarine, melted
2 carrots, shredded
1 small onion, finely chopped
1/4 cup chopped pimiento, optional
1 can (10 3/4 oz.) cream of chicken soup, regular or reduced-fat
1/2 cup sour cream, regular or low-fat

Heat oven to 350°. Spray a 3-quart casserole with nonstick cooking spray. Cover squash with water and cook until tender-crisp. Drain well. Combine dressing mix with melted butter. Combine cooked squash, carrots, onion, pimiento, soup and sour cream. Add 1/2 of the stuffing mixture and stir well. Pour into casserole. Top with remaining stuffing mixture. Bake for 25 minutes.

BAKED CELERY WITH WATER CHESTNUTS

Servings: 10-14

If you enjoy the crunchy texture of celery and water chestnuts, this dish is for you. It goes well with a simple roasted chicken or Cornish hens and makes a nice side dish for a buffet. The recipe can be cut in half.

8 cups celery, cut into 1-inch slices
2 cans (8 oz. each) sliced water chestnuts, drained
2 cans (10¾ oz. each) cream of chicken soup, regular or reduced-fat
½ cup chopped green bell pepper
½ cup toasted slivered almonds
½ cup breadcrumbs
¼ cup butter or margarine, melted

Heat oven to 350°. Spray a 2-quart casserole with nonstick cooking spray. Cook celery in boiling salted water for 6 to 10 minutes or until tender-crisp. Drain well and combine with water chestnuts, soup and green pepper. Pour into casserole. Top with almonds and crumbs. Drizzle with melted butter. Bake for 30 minutes or until golden.

ENGLISH PEA CASSEROLE

This recipe turns everyday green peas into something special. It can be made the day before and refrigerated, making it ideal for entertaining during the holidays. The recipe can be easily doubled.

1 pkg. (10 oz.) frozen peas
2 tbs. butter or margarine
1/2 cup diced onion
1/2 cup diced celery
1/2 cup diced green bell pepper
1 can (10¾ oz.) cream of mushroom
  soup, regular or reduced-fat

1/4 cup milk, whole or 2%
1 can (8 oz.) sliced water chestnuts,
  drained
1/4 cup diced pimiento, optional
1 cup crushed cheese crackers

Lightly butter a 2-quart casserole. Thaw peas. Melt butter in a large skillet over medium-high heat and cook onion, celery and green pepper until soft. Combine all ingredients, except crackers, and pour into casserole. Refrigerate overnight to blend flavors.

Heat oven to 350°. Top casserole with cheese crackers and bake for 30 minutes.

BROCCOLI BAKE

This makes a good addition to a buffet table. The recipe can be made ahead and easily doubled.

1 pkg. (10 oz. each) frozen chopped broccoli, cooked and drained
1 can (10¾ oz.) cream of mushroom soup, regular or reduced-fat
2 eggs, beaten, or egg substitute
1 cup chopped onion
¾ cup mayonnaise, regular or low-fat
1 cup shredded cheddar cheese, regular or low-fat
½ cup Ritz cracker crumbs

Heat oven to 350°. Spray a 2-quart casserole with nonstick cooking spray. Combine all ingredients, except cracker crumbs. Pour into casserole. (Can be refrigerated at this point.) Sprinkle with crackers and bake for 30 minutes.

CLASSIC GREEN BEAN CASSEROLE

Servings: 6

This classic is a favorite for everyone. If you'd like to add more crunch, add a can of drained sliced water chestnuts.

2 pkg. (10 oz. each) frozen French cut green beans, thawed
1 can (10 oz.) cream of mushroom soup, regular or reduced-fat
$1/2$ cup milk, whole or 2%
1 tsp. soy sauce
$1/2$ tsp. pepper
1 can (2.8 oz.) French fried onion rings

Heat oven to 350°. Spray a $1^1/_2$-quart casserole with nonstick cooking spray. Mix together green beans, soup, milk, soy sauce and pepper. Add $1/2$ can of the onions. Pour into casserole. Bake for 30 minutes, top with remaining onions and continue baking for 5 more minutes.

CAN-DO CASSEROLES

Having quick-to-make casserole ingredients on your pantry shelf can be a real advantage. In this chapter you will find tasty casseroles that have many ingredients that come out of cans. They are ideal for boating, camping or potlucks. You need a stove or an insulated container to transport them already cooked.

MEXI CAN-CAN CASSEROLE

Servings: 12

Everything but the cheese for this recipe comes out of cans, so it's easy to have all the ingredients ready on your pantry shelf. A great take-along dish for camping or boating, you can assemble it the night before or bake it right away. It feeds a multitude and everyone seems to like it. Serve with chopped onions and sour cream to go on top.

1 can (16 oz.) chili con carne, any liquid drained
1 can (16 oz.) pitted olives, drained
1 can (16 oz.) creamed corn
1 can (16 oz.) whole kernel corn, well drained
3 cans (16 oz. each) prepared tamales, cut into 1-inch pieces
1 lb. cheddar cheese, shredded (can be low-fat)

Spray a 4-quart casserole with nonstick cooking spray. In casserole, combine all ingredients, except ¼ of the cheese. Top with reserved cheese. Refrigerate overnight or bake immediately.

Heat oven to 350°. Bake casserole for 45 minutes.

HAMBURGER HODGEPODGE

The kids seem to go for this quick and easy supper.

1 1/2 lb. lean ground beef
1 cup chopped onion
2 cloves garlic, minced
3 cans (10 oz. each) minestrone soup
1 can (16 oz.) garbanzo beans, rinsed and drained
1 can (31 oz.) pork and beans
1 1/2 cups chopped celery
1 tbs. Worcestershire sauce
1 tsp. crumbled oregano flakes

Heat oven to 350°. In a large skillet over medium-high heat, cook ground beef, onion and garlic until beef is browned. Drain off any excess liquid or fat. In a large bowl, combine beef mixture with remaining ingredients. Pour into a shallow 3-quart casserole. Bake for 45 minutes.

CITRUS-BAKED FRUIT

Serve this colorful casserole as a winter brunch.

3 oranges
3 lemons
1/2 cup brown sugar
2 cans (1 lb. each) apricot halves, drained
2 cans (1 lb. each) pineapple chunks, drained
2 cans (1 lb. each) sliced peaches, drained
1 tsp. nutmeg
1 cup sour cream, regular or low-fat, for topping

Heat oven to 325°. Grate zest of 1 orange and 1 lemon. Set fruits aside for another use. Combine grated zest with brown sugar. Cut remaining 2 oranges and 2 lemons into paper-thin slices. (A food processor works well for this.) Leave skin on fruit. Layer canned fruits and citrus slices alternately with brown sugar mixture in a shallow 2-quart casserole. Top with grated nutmeg. Bake for 20 minutes or until hot and bubbly. Serve warm with a dollop of sour cream.

TUNA AND CASHEW CASSEROLE

This one is a snap to put together. Save 1/2 cup of the noodles for the top.

1 can (4 oz.) chow mein noodles
1 can (10¾ oz.) mushroom soup, regular or reduced-fat
¼ cup milk
1 can (6 oz.) tuna packed in water, drained
1 cup chopped celery
¼ cup chopped onion
1 cup cashew nuts
salt and pepper to taste

Heat oven to 325°. Spray a 1½-quart casserole with nonstick cooking spray. Reserve ½ cup of the noodles for topping. Combine remaining ingredients in a bowl and pour into casserole. Sprinkle top with remaining noodles. Bake for 25 minutes.

CORNED BEEF CASSEROLE

Servings: 4-6

You can use corned beef from a can or the deli for this casserole. It has real stick-to-your-ribs goodness and has been a family favorite for many years.

1 can (12 oz.) corned beef, chopped
4 oz. American cheese, finely diced
1 can (10¾ oz.) cream of chicken soup, regular or reduced-fat
1 cup milk
½ cup chopped onion
6 oz. dried macaroni, cooked and drained
¼ cup soft breadcrumbs
2 tbs. butter or margarine, melted

Heat oven to 375°. Spray a 2-quart casserole with nonstick cooking spray. Combine corned beef, cheese, soup, milk and onion in a large bowl. Layer cooked macaroni with corned beef mixture twice. Top with crumbs and drizzle with butter. Bake for 1 hour.

SWEET POTATO BAKE

Servings: 6-8

This great tasting dish couldn't be easier to prepare—just open the cans and combine in a pretty casserole dish. It's a wonderful dish to take along to a holiday party, because no one will guess you didn't go to a lot of trouble.

2 cans (18 oz.) sweet potatoes or yams
1 can (21 oz.) apple pie filling
1 can (18 oz.) whole cranberries
2 tbs. orange marmalade
2 tbs. apricot jam

Heat oven to 350°. Place sweet potatoes in a 1½-quart casserole dish and top with apple pie filling and cranberries. Gently stir to combine. Combine marmalade and apricot jam and spread over the top. Bake for 30 to 40 minutes or until bubbly.

CALICO BEANS

These beans are nice to take along on a picnic—keep warm in one of those insulated casserole bags.

1 lb. lean ground beef
1/2 lb. bacon, diced
1 cup chopped onion
1 tsp. salt
3/4 cup brown sugar, packed
1 tsp. dry mustard
2 tsp. cider vinegar
1 can (16 oz.) pork and beans
1 can (10 oz.) garbanzo beans, rinsed and
   drained
1 can (16 oz.) kidney beans, rinsed and drained
1 can (16 oz.) lima beans, rinsed and drained

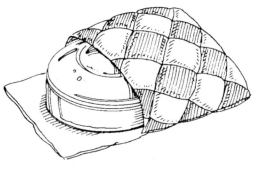

Heat oven to 350°. In a large skillet over medium-high heat, brown beef with bacon and onion. Drain off fat. Combine with remaining ingredients and place in a 3-quart casserole. Bake for 45 minutes.

SCALLOPED CORN AND TOMATO BAKE

Servings: 8-12

Enjoy this savory pudding on Thanksgiving or other holidays—or anytime!

2 cans (14 oz.) tomatoes, drained and chopped
1 can (15 oz.) whole kernel corn, drained
1 can (14 oz.) cream-style corn
2 eggs, beaten (can be egg substitute)
1/4 cup flour

1 tbs. sugar
1 tsp. pepper
1 onion, finely chopped
1/2 tsp. garlic powder
1/3 cup butter or margarine
2 cups soft breadcrumbs
1/2 cup grated Parmesan cheese

Heat oven to 350°. Spray a 2-quart casserole with nonstick cooking spray. Stir together tomatoes, corn, cream-style corn, eggs, flour, sugar and pepper. Pour into casserole. In a skillet over medium-high heat, melt butter and sauté onion until soft. Combine with garlic powder, crumbs and Parmesan and sprinkle on top of the casserole. Bake for 1 hour.

INDEX

Serve Creative, Easy, Nutritious Meals with nitty gritty® Cookbooks

100 Dynamite Desserts
The 9 x 13 Pan Cookbook
The Barbecue Cookbook *(new)*
Beer and Good Food
The Best Bagels are Made at Home
The Best Pizza is Made at Home*(new)*
Bread Baking
Bread Machine Cookbook
Bread Machine Cookbook II
Bread Machine Cookbook III
Bread Machine Cookbook IV
Bread Machine Cookbook V
Bread Machine Cookbook VI
Cappuccino/Espresso
Casseroles *(new)*
The Coffee Book
Convection Oven Cookery *(new)*
Cooking for 1 or 2
Cooking in Clay
Cooking in Porcelain
Cooking with Chile Peppers
Cooking with Grains
Cooking with Your Kids
Creative Mexican Cooking
Deep Fried Indulgences

The Dehydrator Cookbook
Easy Vegetarian Cooking
Edible Pockets for Every Meal
Entrées From Your Bread Machine
Extra-Special Crockery Pot Recipes
Fabulous Fiber Cookery
Fondue and Hot Dips
Fresh Vegetables
From Freezer, 'Fridge and Pantry
From Your Ice Cream Maker
The Garlic Cookbook
Gourmet Gifts
Healthy Cooking on the Run
Healthy Snacks for Kids
Indoor Grilling
The Juicer Book
The Juicer Book II
Lowfat American Favorites
Marinades
Muffins, Nut Breads and More
The New Blender Book
New International Fondue Cookbook
No Salt, No Sugar, No Fat
One-Dish Meals
Oven and Rotisserie Roasting

Party Fare
The Pasta Machine Cookbook
Pinch of Time: Meals in Less than 30
  Minutes
Quick and Easy Pasta Recipes
Recipes for the Loaf Pan
Recipes for the Pressure Cooker
Recipes for Yogurt Cheese
Risottos, Paellas, and other Rice
  Specialties
The Sandwich Maker Cookbook
The Sensational Skillet: Sautés and
  Stir-Fries *(new)*
Slow Cooking in Crock-Pot,® Slow
  Cooker, Oven and Multi-Cooker
The Steamer Cookbook
The Toaster Oven Cookbook
Unbeatable Chicken Recipes
The Versatile Rice Cooker
Waffles
The Well Dressed Potato
The Wok
Worldwide Sourdoughs from Your
  Bread Machine
Wraps and Roll-Ups

For a free catalog, call: Bristol Publishing Enterprises, Inc.
(800) 346-4889
www.bristolcookbooks.com